THE PARADOX OF WORSHIP

THE PARADOX OF WORSHIP

Michael Perry

LONDON

SPCK

First published 1977
SPCK
Holy Trinity Church
Marylebone Road
London NW1 4DU

BV10.2

847

Printed in Great Britain by
The Camelot Press Ltd, Southampton

ISBN 0 281 02973 3

To
MERLIN AND KATHLEEN
gratefully

CONTENTS

ACKNOWLEDGEMENTS

My thanks go to the following, for granting permission to make use of material of which they own or administer the copyright:

A. & C. Black Ltd: *The Shape of the Liturgy*, by Dom Gregory Dix.

Wm Collins Sons & Co. Ltd: *Good News in Galatians*, by John D. Davies.

Darton, Longman & Todd Ltd: *The Language of the Rite*, by Roger Grainger.

Faber & Faber Ltd: *God was in Christ*, by D. M. Baillie.

Hodder & Stoughton Ltd and the Bethany Fellowship Inc.: *The Charismatic Prayer Group*, by John Gunstone.

A. R. Mowbray & Co. Ltd: *The Fourth Dimension*, by A. D. Duncan.

Oxford University Press: *The Idea of the Holy*, by Rudolf Otto, tr. John W. Harvey.

S.C.M. Press Ltd: *Anglican Public Worship*, by Colin Dunlop.

The Seabury Press Inc.: *The Rhythm of God: A Philosophy of Worship*, by Geddes MacGregor. Copyright © 1974 by The Seabury Press, Inc., New York. Used by permission.

The Society for Promoting Christian Knowledge: *Durham Essays and Addresses*, by Michael Ramsey; *The Eucharist Today: Studies on Series 3*, ed. R. C. D. Jasper; articles by J. M. Lochman and John Riches in *Theology*.

Times Newspapers Ltd: 'Understanding the mystery of the Christian Church', by Michael Richards, in *The Times*, 28 December 1974.

The United Society for the Propagation of the Gospel: *Thinking Mission 5*, by Margaret Dewey.

Extracts from the New English Bible, second edition © 1970, are used by permission of Oxford and Cambridge University Presses.

Extracts from *Alternative Services, Third Series*, An Order for Holy Communion, are reproduced by permission of S.P.C.K. on behalf of the Provinces of Canterbury and York.

PREFACE

The following pages contain an expanded version of the Selwyn Lectures for 1976, delivered at St John's College Auckland and in various other places in New Zealand. Parts of the first chapter also formed the 1976 B. R. Marshall Memorial Lecture in Trinity College Chapel, Melbourne.

For some time now, I have wanted to reflect theologically on what is happening when Christians come together for worship, and these lectureships made me set aside time to do so. I should like to thank the several nominators for honouring me with their invitations.

The time I spent in New Zealand (both within the friendly and accepting community of St John's College and at the homes of so many different people) has laid up a store of happy memories which will last a very long time indeed, and the same is true of my journey out and back again. I have been amazed and humbled by the ready hospitality both of so many old friends and of so many newly-made ones. Their names are too many to be individually included in a brief preface, but I cannot forbear particular mention of Merlin and Kathleen Davies, to whom my debt (which goes back to the very beginnings of my ordained ministry) is beyond words.

Finally, my only regret is that so little has been made of so vast a field, and that so many topics which might have been taken up have not had so much as a mention. My only defence is to say that I believe the subject to be so important that even the selective treatment it here receives need not be despised, if it can but help stimulate the reader to reflect more deeply for himself on the great mystery of Christian worship.

The College, Durham   MICHAEL PERRY
August 1976

FURTHER READING

This book has not been provided with a bibliography. Readers who wish to follow up any of the subjects raised will find ample help in the books and articles listed in the Notes which follow Chapter 5.

1

WORSHIP AND
GOD

What is happening when Christians worship? That is an apparently
simple question, but the answer is not as straightforward as we might
think. I want to ask that question and begin to explore ways of
answering it, because I believe that, as we do so, we shall be led first
to a dilemma and then to a discovery.

The dilemma comes because we can approach the question from
two possible directions, but in each case we soon find ourselves in
difficulties, and eventually we have to confess that we appear to have
started from the wrong place. The discovery comes when we admit
the dilemma. It is that the clue to illuminate our whole understanding
of Christian worship cannot be found by avoiding the dilemma but only
by admitting it. The dilemma is not only inescapable; it is indispensable.

There are two possible directions from which we may approach
the question, 'What is happening when Christians worship?' If we
want to explore the first of these, the *Shorter Oxford English
Dictionary* is a useful place to begin. That tome tells us that the word
'worship' means 'reverence or veneration paid to a being or power
regarded as supernatural or divine' and that it derives from an Old
English word meaning 'worth-ship'. True enough; trite enough. We
have been taught from Sunday School days onwards that
worshipping is ascribing worth to God. But let us look at that idea.
We may find that it leads us in an unexpected—and not entirely
acceptable—direction.

We look at ourselves and discover that we are of very limited
worth. We are full of human inadequacies and inconsistencies. We
are to a large extent the victims of our heredity and upbringing. We
have only a limited ability to cope either with the demands of the
world outside, or the buffets of fortune or misfortune, or the
irrationalities which lurk not far below the surface of that polished

1

mask of urbane humanity which we put on when we face the world. If we are religious men, though, we believe that there is a power, behind and beyond the surface of things seen, which is greater than the human. It is a power which transcends human limitations and can overrule the misfortunes which overpower mere humanity. As worshippers, we believe we can enter into relations with that superhuman power. As *Christian* worshippers, we *know* we can, because we know that power as personal and as revealed to mankind in the figure of Jesus the Christ. So, in our worship, we ascribe the due and proper worth to that God with whom we are entering into relations. In worship, we transcend our own human limitations and imperfections by linking ourselves with the supernatural power behind the universe.

Christian worship includes a number of activities. When the Christian worships, he adores, he confesses, he gives thanks, he makes requests, and he intercedes. Each of these activities can be seen in terms of ascribing to God his proper worth. As the Christian worshipper *adores*, he realizes the power, the otherness, the sheer numinous holiness of God. He ascribes those qualities to him, so that he may the more strongly realize God's worth. As he *confesses* his sins, he measures his own worthlessness against the worth of God and acknowledges this, lest God's holy wrath shrivel him up as a reward for his presumption in daring to come too close. As he *gives thanks*, he realizes that whatever comes to him, comes from God's hand, and he lets the truth that God is the sovereign dispenser of all things, penetrate his thinking and guide his actions. As he *makes requests* of God, both for himself and for others, he ascribes to God the worth of the being who is creator and giver of all. God is the person who can hand us the things that we want, so it behoves us to ask him for them.

Can you see what is happening as we explore the implications of this prevalent idea of worship as 'ascribing worth to God'? Somehow, the flavour is coming out all wrong. There seems to be a calculatedness to it which is leading us in the wrong direction altogether. The 'thrust', the emphasis, is on the benefits secured for the worshipper. God provides those benefits, and his worth must be acknowledged, but our eyes are focusing increasingly on the gifts, whilst the Giver is in danger of becoming little more than a means towards an end.

The direction in which we are being impelled is towards a magical rather than a religious relation between God and ourselves. Both the magician and the man of religion believe in the existence of superhuman powers and in the possibility of man's entering into relations with them. Both the magician and the man of religion wish to ascribe to these powers their true worth. But from that point on, their attitudes are diametrically opposed, and as a result the worth ascribed is of a very different character.

A magician wants to use the supernatural forces for his own ends. He certainly does not initiate these forces; nor can he control them, for their power is greater than his, and it is not entirely predictable. What he aims to do is to manipulate or channel these forces, or deflect them so that they act where and how he wants them to act, and so that they serve his own purposes. To some extent the magician is a technologist. As the technologist seeks to harness the forces of nature and make them work for him, so the magician seeks to harness the forces of supernature. Aladdin's relation to the genie of the lamp is a relation of this sort. He ascribes worth to the genie. He knows that the genie wields a great deal of power. He knows, also, that if he is not careful, the genie will get the better of him. What Aladdin has to do is to exercise sufficient cunning so that, weak and human though he is, he can yet control the powerful genie. His relation to it will include adoration, thanksgiving, petition, and intercession. He will realize the genie's power and otherness, he will thank him for what he has done (even though Aladdin's attitude has more in it of buttering-up than of genuine gratitude), he will ask him to do things both for himself and for others; but his worship of the genie will be very far indeed from a Christian's worship of his God. The Christian does not see the superhuman forces as a challenge to his wits and ingenuity. Rather, he sees them as the manifestation of the actions of a person—a person whom he tries, not to outwit, but to co-operate with. This person, his God, he recognizes as a God of sovereign freedom and absolute power, and he seeks to align himself with his purposes and to treat him as Lord and master. This is why Christian worship has an entirely different 'feel' to it from Aladdin's worship of the genie of the lamp.

It is becoming clear that this idea of 'ascribing worth' is a dangerous one. It sounds noble, spiritual and God-directed, but it can so easily degenerate into something almost entirely man-centred. We start with the idea of God's worth or value. That soon becomes, not God's worth in himself, but his value to us. It is man and his needs which are becoming the criteria of the value and effectiveness of worship.

We can see this beginning to happen when (as is so often the case) we try to assess an act of worship in terms of how effectively it has taught a particular doctrine, or how well-chosen the hymns have been for the purpose of ramming home the message of the sermon. This is a particularly insidious perversion and there can be few of us who have not been guilty of it at some time or other. It is a perversion because it treats worship, not as an activity whose justification is to be sought solely in itself and by its own inherent criteria, but as something which has to justify itself by the criteria of quite another discipline. In this case, it is the discipline of education which is given priority. An act of worship is felt to have 'succeeded' if a message or a doctrine has been so clearly articulated in the course of it that the worshippers are firmer in their grasp of that aspect of Christian truth after the service than before. The prayers may still technically be addressed to God, but they are selected according to their probable effect on the congregation; the same applies to the other parts of the service. When this happens, it is not worship we are planning but instruction. As Colin Dunlop warned us a generation ago, the person who does this 'has failed to justify public worship: he has merely succeeded in employing the time formerly occupied by public worship in doing something else.'[1]

It would be easy to see this as an overspill into adult worship of attitudes proper to the worship of the Sunday School, were it not for the fact that it is as out of place in the Sunday School as in the adult congregation. Neither for adults nor for children should worship be prostituted to pedagogy. 'That is not to say that liturgy, like other forms of art, cannot accomplish any teaching mission. Of course it can and it must; but the teaching must be indirect. . . . Even the faintest suggestion of schoolmastering is ruinous to the rhythm of God' (Geddes MacGregor).[2]

Roger Grainger, in his recent book *The Language of the Rite*, believes that we have Calvin to blame for this over-intellectualist attitude which subordinates worship to instruction. The Reformers put a heavy premium on intellectual clarity because they believed that the symbolism of the sacraments did not shine by its own light but required verbal explanation before it could be trusted to give the right message to the worshippers.

> The sacraments . . . mediate not the presence of God, but His message to men. Their value consists in their being explained and explicable. 'The word when preached,' says Calvin, 'makes us understand what the visible sign means.' . . . Everywhere, explanation creeps in to destroy the symbol. . . . Instead of being the unknowable in its own form of knowledge, the Word made flesh for men, the sacrament appears as an explicit message about God out of scripture, the bread and wine being reduced to a mere 'visual aid' to the intelligence of the worshipper.[3]

Worship thus becomes over-intellectualized, and the flesh, materiality, 'is not so much redeemed and restored as denied and dismissed'.[4] Worshippers begin to expect quite the wrong things of it. They ask, 'What have I learnt today?', instead of thinking of the central concern of corporate worship as 'the presence, coming, challenge, and claim of God'.[5] Our aim should be, not the perfectly-instructed congregation, but 'a worshipping congregation so fully and desperately involved in playing out the Liturgy that it would communicate . . . a sense of the wonder, the joy, and the mystery of God' (Neville Clark).[6]

There are other snags in this idea of worship as 'ascribing worth to God'. A man can do this only if he believes in God and has been caught hold of by a conviction of his existence and attributes. There are some people to whom belief comes easily, and who habitually enjoy those feelings of numinous satisfaction which they associate with what they call a 'good' act of worship. Most of us are not made like that. The more typical twentieth-century Western man has a struggle to reach belief. He is often not very sure whether there is a God or not. Even when he *is* sure, he does not always feel a compulsion to express his convictions through worship, and there are many times for him when the hour of worship brings him no very profound feelings to enjoy. For that sort of a man, the idea of 'ascribing worth' brings scant comfort. If this is all worship is, it is hard not to feel that the whole enterprise would better be shelved altogether during those times of intellectual doubt or spiritual dryness which come from time to time to almost all of us.

Why is it that we run into difficulties when we start with the idea of worship as 'ascribing worth to God'? I would submit that it is because we are beginning at the wrong point. We think of worship as primarily a human activity. It may be directed towards a superhuman end, but all the same, it is an activity which human beings initiate. It is hard therefore not to make human needs, human feelings, human understanding, and human attitudes determinative.

— ▶▼◀ —

In this case, can we understand worship more satisfactorily if we try another point of entry? I think we can. I still think we shall get into difficulties, but I think we shall get further before they begin to become obvious.

The last time, we began with a very human book—the *Shorter Oxford English Dictionary*. This time, let us begin with a book of a very different character—by looking at some examples of worship as it presents itself to us in the pages of the Bible.

Jacob on the run from his brother Esau (Gen. 28.10–19) was, perhaps, imagining that as he got out of range of his revengeful family so he would also get out of range of the family God. But in his exhaustion he stopped for the night and dreamed. In his dream, the traffic between heaven and earth became luminously visible for that brief moment of supernatural awareness, and when he woke up, he was constrained to cry out 'How fearsome is this place!' and to set up a stone altar to be a place for the commerce between man and God. Jacob did not initiate the worship, any more than the subsequent worshippers at that place did. The worship was there before Jacob became aware of it. At the place which used to be called Luz but which had thenceforth to be known as The House of God (Beth-El) he had his eyes opened to the heavenly worship, to the ladder full of angels going up and down between heaven and earth, who

wait around him, ready still
To sing his praise and do his will.

The theological term is 'prevenience', meaning that the action of God precedes in every way the response which it makes possible. When Jacob's vision had faded into the cold light of common day, he set up an altar as a response to what had been already *there* and which had been unseen and unrecognized until God had revealed his secrets to the patriarch. The worshippers who gathered thereafter at Beth-El were joining in an activity which antedated their presence and which would be going on unseen whether they offered human worship or not.

The same sense of the divine prevenience in worship is to be seen in the vision of Isaiah 6. Isaiah discovered that the place of Israelite worship was also a place where Jahveh sat, high and exalted, with the skirt of his robe filling the Temple, surrounded by six-winged creatures ceaselessly crying to one another and calling 'Holy, Holy, Holy'.

The writer who is responsible for the final form of the book called Exodus had the same belief. The details of the worship of the sanctuary were not a matter for human choice. The way things were to be done was according to God's specification, made known by him to Moses. Look, for example, at Exodus 25—30. 'The LORD spoke to Moses and said: . . . Make me a sanctuary, and I will dwell among them. Make it exactly according to the design I show you'—and then there follow chapter after chapter of specifications for the Ark, the table of acacia-wood, the lamp-stand, the Tabernacle and its hangings and furnishings. The same is true of the details of the vestments for Aaron and his sons, and the ritual to be observed at their installation as priests. All of it was appointed directly by Jahveh, and the act of consecration—though outwardly performed by Moses—was really the action of God himself. '*I* shall hallow the Tent of the Presence and the altar; and Aaron and his sons *I* shall consecrate to serve me as priests' (Exod. 29.44). Worship is God's business, both in principle and in its details. As the writer of the Epistle to the Hebrews was to say of another altar in a later age, the human altar was a copy and shadow or pattern or figure or symbol or parable (Heb. 8.5; 9.9, 23, 24; 10.1) of the true, pre-existent,

eternal, heavenly one. 'Like the shadows in Plato's cave, the
sacrificial order tells us something about how things are in the archetypical realm of which the earthly tabernacle is but a mirroring'.[7]

Or again, we may instance the way in which the men of Israel kept
their Passover, dipping their fingers in the bitter herbs as they joined
in their festival of worship. They did not believe they were celebrating
a human *in*vention, but that they were placing themselves once more
at the place of divine *inter*vention, when God rescued and redeemed
the people he had called as his own. When Jews celebrate Passover, it
is as if the act of remembrance takes them back in time so that they
become the contemporaries of those slaves of old who were delivered
from Egyptian bondage by God's mighty act. The same is more
significantly true of the Christian antitype of the Passover, the
Eucharist in which the worshipper identifies himself by joining in the
eternal sacrifice of the Son of God and places himself anew each time
at the pivotal point of history, showing forth the death of the Lord till
he comes (1 Cor. 11.26). Making *anamnesis* of Jesus in the Eucharist
is a recalling, a re-calling, a calling of Jesus out of the past into the
present. Yet this re-calling does not depend on the vividness of our
imagination but on the promise of God. 'We are taken, by the power
of the Holy Spirit, into the presence of the living Jesus. We become
present once again at those sacred and eternal moments of past
history', at the time and the place of the one, perfect, and sufficient
sacrifice, oblation, and satisfaction for the sins of the whole
world—a sacrifice which can never be repeated but which can
always be entered into.[8] *We* do not perform the Eucharist; we only
arrange the conditions so that *God* can make the eternal sacrifice
effective at this moment in time and this spot in space. And even the
conditions are not ours, but given us by God!

A final example of the same thing may be seen in that description
in Acts 2.42–7 of the life and worship of the infant Church soon after
the feast of Pentecost. We read that

> they met constantly to hear the apostles teach, and to share the
> common life, to break bread, and to pray. . . . With one mind they
> kept up their daily attendance at the temple, and, breaking bread
> in private houses, shared their meals with unaffected joy, as they

praised God and enjoyed the favour of the whole people. And day by day the Lord added to their number those whom he was saving.

We shall be seeing in later chapters that there are strong links between belief, worship, community, and mission. The immediately obvious connection is that shared beliefs lead to common worship and that this knits into community and creates mission. Thus, in the example from Acts which we have just taken, the disciples held beliefs about God and his relation to Jesus of Nazareth which distinguished them from mainstream Judaism. These beliefs they expressed in their common worship, particularly in their frequent coming together for the Breaking of Bread. These shared beliefs not only differentiated them from the majority of their religious fellow-countrymen; they also helped to create a bond of fellowship between them as the community of those people who shared the secret of God's newly-declared purpose. They banded together, therefore, for mutual support and encouragement. Their community was so close that 'all whose faith had drawn them together held everything in common: they would sell their property and possessions and make a general distribution as the need of each required'. As a result of this fellowship, they were an attractive and an attracting community, so that their missionary endeavours were rewarded by a daily expansion of their numbers.

That is the immediately obvious connection between belief, worship, community, and mission, and it is obvious to the outsider as well as to the Christian. There is truth in it, certainly—but only a small part of the truth, and by far the least significant. The outsider believes he has seen everything when he sees the disciples propounding this novel and minority theology in such a way that they are impelled to offer a worship which creates a strong bond of fellowship and attracts an increasing crowd of supporters. But the outsider is satisfied with a very partial view of things because he cannot see the prevenient activity of God in the whole process, not only in belief, community, and mission, but also in worship.

Belief is not the result of human ratiocination. Reason does not create belief, though natural theology has an important corroborative function. Belief is what happens when God reveals the truth about himself to a man so that his heart and mind are opened to accept the truth of that revelation which has come to him. *Community*, fellowship, in the Christian sense, is more than men with similar ideas and ideals clubbing together to make a united front, as they might do for a railway preservation society or a stamp-collecting club. Christian fellowship, *koinonia*, is God calling out men whom he has chosen to be the bearers of his truth before the nations, God building up his Church, the body of his Christ, the community of men and women who know that Christ has said to them, 'You did not choose me: I chose you' (John 15.16). Likewise with *mission*. Mission is not what a man does to win converts to his cause as though they were to be adherents of one or other rival political parties. Mission (or at all events part of mission, for we shall be seeing in Chapter 4 that mission is wider than evangelism)—mission is '*The Lord* [adding] to their number those whom *he* [is] saving' (Acts 2.47). And just as the divine priority can be asserted in belief, community, and mission, so it can be in the case of worship. Worship is not a human activity directed *at* God, but a divine activity initiated *by* God, in which we are privileged to share. God *draws* men to worship with him; the Father *seeks* people to worship him in spirit and in truth (John 4.23—A.V. and R.S.V. have the flavour of the Greek *zetei* better than N.E.B.'s 'whom the Father wants').

Worship is a divine activity. When God reveals his nature and purposes to men, and they engage in worship, they are taking part in something which existed before them and which would be going on whether they joined in it or not. To quote Colin Dunlop,

> An individual Christian coming to church comes not so much to offer worship as to join in an offering continually going on. He comes not to initiate worship but to contribute to, and be carried up by, a worship which never ceases, the source and fountain of which lies in the eternal activity of Christ.[9]

Worship is an activity of the Holy Trinity, an activity which does not depend on human awareness or human participation, but which is entirely prevenient. Indeed, as Dunlop went on to say, the doctrine of the Holy Trinity is deeply implied in any possible analysis of the nature of worship. Because it is only through the Holy Spirit that we can have faith in Christ and because only in Christ can we approach the Father, all prayer and worship is a sharing in the life of God. Within the Being of God there is love given and love received, adoration offered and adoration accepted. When Christians worship, they are drawn into this timeless and eternal activity, which goes on whether they join in or not. In worship we are taken up into God and allowed to live His life.[10]

The sense of this is brought out in the famous quotation from the Venerable Bede in his monastic community at Jarrow thirteen hundred years ago. When Alcuin was writing to the community at Wearmouth, he reminded them that

> it is told how blessed Bede, our master and your patron, said 'I know that the angels are present at the canonical Hours, and what if they do not find me among the brethren when they assemble? Will they not say, Where is Bede?'[11]

Worship is God's business. It is not we who baptize or celebrate the Eucharist; even weddings (so they say) are made in heaven. It is *Christ* who baptizes and adds new members to his Body; it is *Christ* who is the unseen President at every Eucharist, present in his Body and his Blood. Worship, community, and mission are closely inter-related, but the inter-relation which we saw a few pages back as being obvious to the outsider is only a superficial inter-relation. That had worship as the cause and community and mission as the effects. The relationship in fact is a far closer one. All three are aspects of the same thing. Worship is an activity of God, fellowship is an expression of being Christ's Body, and mission is the nature of the God whose activity we join when we worship and whose Body we are if he has called us.

This approach to worship is leading us in a very different direction from that of the 'ascribing worth to God' starting-point. As it starts from the divine side, the sovereign independence of God is determinative of the whole understanding and practice of worship which stems from it. We still adore and thank, we still intercede and make petition, but the flavour is different. *Adoration* and *contemplation* are content to accept the understanding of God which he has revealed to the worshipping heart. Like Jean Louis Chaffengeon, the old man who spent his days at the back of the church at Ars, the worshipper says only, 'I look at him. He looks at me'.[12] *Thanksgiving* is more conscious of God than of his gifts. The sole aim of the worshipper is to align himself with the divine will and purpose, so that *intercession* and *petition* are controlled by a sense of 'not my will but thine be done' (Luke 22.42).

Yet this understanding of worship is not without its pitfalls. To them we must now turn.

1.   If we go over completely to this viewpoint, we shall be overstating a case and losing some undoubted truths which can be expressed along the lines of 'ascribing worth to God'. There *is* a human aspect to worship, and it *is* a right and proper thing to do to respond out of the fulness of our hearts to what we see and know of God.

2.   If we think of worship as something entirely initiated by God, into the constant stream of which we insert our own echoes of the divine activity, we are in danger of forgetting that worship is something at which we have to *work* and which demands human effort of us. We do not simply relax into worship, nor do we only engage in it at the rare times when we are particularly conscious of the overarching and prevenient work of God. As Geddes MacGregor points out,

> Some Christians have felt the sense of that prevenience so vividly that they have accounted the proper attitude toward God to be nothing other than a silent waiting. Such an attitude, which historians of Christian mystical piety call Quietism, fails fully to appreciate the nature of adoring love. Genuine love does not wait frigidly for the lover to woo but goes forth in loving response, confidently knowing that the lover is already on his way.[13]

3.   This approach to worship tends to go together with a liturgical conservatism. There can be the attitude that the classical liturgy of the past (whether it be the Tridentine Mass in the Latin tongue or the

Elizabethan cadences of the Book of Common Prayer) came down from heaven in the same way as those Old Testament rituals in Exodus 25—30 at which we were looking a few pages back, and that it is therefore impious to try to alter or replace them. They are old and tried and safe, and they speak to us of God the great and unchanging Rock of Ages:

> O strength and stay upholding all creation,
> Who ever dost thyself unmoved abide.

People who think this way believe that it is a very unsafe thing to try and concoct a new liturgy, because in the making cf it we are likely to be far more conscious of the efforts of man and the rival factions in the Synod which has to approve it, than of the guiding hand of God. Logically, conservatism ought not to follow from an insistence that our worship is the shadow of God's divine worship, because God's action is, supremely, unpredictable. The Spirit blows where he lists and often catches us completely unawares. In practice, however, this point is not taken as often as it might be.

4. A final danger in making the divine aspect the sole and determinative way of approaching an understanding of worship is pointed out by Roger Grainger, following a hint from Louis Bouyer. It is that it would destroy the sacramental balance of human and divine. There is danger in embracing *either* extreme. On behalf of the 'human' aspect of worship, Grainger says that

> if the movement of men towards God is in fact natural to mankind, if it is a natural instinct of worship, a native sacrality, however imperfect, then it must constitute a part of that humanness which was perfected by the Incarnation. It must be at least potentially good; it must always be held to have a value of its own; and the notion of its value must be preserved.[14]

That, however, does not mean that it is safe to go over entirely to the 'human' pole. If we did so, we would be sacralizing all things human in a way which denied the truth and significance of the 'natural' division between sacred and profane; it would be tantamount to saying that 'man himself, rather than man as he turns to God, is naturally sacred, and his worship is simply the expression of his divinity'.[15] And yet it is as grievous an error to move to the opposite pole and suppose that the sacraments owe nothing of their significance to any human element whatever.

> Both attitudes (Bouyer distinguishes them as the Nestorian and Monophysite heresies) are equally misguided; for the action of Divinity is to redeem and restore human truth rather than to replace it: 'The Incarnation does not lead to the disappearance of natural sacredness, but to its metamorphosis.' Man is not swallowed up by God in Christ, but met and transformed through Him.[16]

We have explored the two ways of approach to our initial question of the relationship between man and God in worship, and our difficulty is obvious. Neither way is without its difficulties, and neither by itself could be tolerated as a full description of the transaction between man and God which is Christian worship. Yet each seems to preserve insights which are valid and of which we ought not to lose sight. How are we to find a way off the horns of this dilemma? It is at this point that we make our discovery, and it is a discovery which shows that we have done right to press the positive advantages of each approach as far as they will go; because the discovery is that our solution will never be found by some kind of half-way mediating position between the two approaches. It will only be found in a transcending inclusiveness which takes both approaches simultaneously as far as they will go. As with Alice, both must win and both should have prizes; not by denying but by including the other. This inclusiveness demands that we allow the nature of worship and the relation of God to man within it to be a paradox.

We ought not to be worried by this. Paradox is close to the heart of many a Christian doctrine. It is constant and ubiquitous within Christian theology. That seminal book of Donald Baillie's, *God was in Christ*, showed us how 'Christian faith, when thought out, conceptualized, and put into human language, runs into paradox . . . at every vital point'.[17] It is true of the doctrine of creation, it is true of the doctrine of providence, it is true of what Baillie called 'the central paradox', the paradox of grace, that particularly crucial 'clue to the understanding of that perfect life in which the paradox is complete and absolute, that life of Jesus which, being the perfection of humanity, is also, and even in a deeper and prior sense, the very life of God Himself'.[18] It is to the paradox of grace, the relation between divine grace and human effort, that the paradox of worship is most closely related. This is not surprising, for 'the very act of worship, particularly corporate worship, involves the use of words and thoughts about God, and to think or speak of God at all is to run into antinomy, dialectical contradiction, paradox'.[19]

The text which Donald Baillie believed illustrated most vividly the paradox of grace was 1 Corinthians 15.10: 'By God's grace I am what I am, nor has his grace been given to me in vain; on the contrary, in my labours I have outdone them all—not I, indeed, but the grace of God working with me.' The exact text on which to base the doctrine does not matter, for it can be found expressed on page after page of the writings of Paul. It is to be found in Galatians 2.20—'I have been crucified with Christ; yet I live; and yet no longer I, but Christ liveth in me' (R.V.). It is to be found in Philippians 2.12 f: 'You must work out your own salvation in fear and trembling; for it is God who works in you. . . .'

> Its essence lies in the conviction which a Christian man possesses, that every good thing in him, every good thing he does, is somehow not wrought by himself but by God. This is a highly paradoxical conviction, for in ascribing all to God it does not abrogate human personality nor disclaim personal responsibility. Never is human action more truly and fully personal, never does the agent feel more perfectly free, than in those moments of which he can say as a Christian that whatever good was in them was not his but God's.[20]

If this is true of grace and goodness it is also true of worship. We worship by the Spirit of God (Phil. 3.3 N.E.B. mg.), in spirit and in truth (John 4.23)—the Spirit he has given us (1 John 3.24) to inspire both the will and the deed, for his own chosen purpose (Phil. 2.13). We must therefore work out our own worship in fear and trembling, for it is God who worships in us. I worship; yet no longer I, but Christ worships in me.

The solution of the dilemma about the human and the divine initiative in worship lies not, therefore, in an either/or, or in a central mediating position, but in a both/and. We do not have to choose between treating worship as a divine or a human activity; we will not begin to understand it properly until we see it as an activity in which both man and God have their parts. The divine part is possible because the Christian God is God the Holy Trinity, and in that Trinity the humanity of Christ has been taken within the deity; the human part is likewise only possible because worship is offered in the Spirit and through Jesus the Son, himself both God and man and therefore the only mediator between things human and things divine.

The human part of the paradoxically divine/human activity of worship is a part which will take all our effort, all our care, all our thought, all our planning. It may be true (as we shall be seeing in Chapter 4) that worship expresses and effects the *mission* of God. That does not absolve us from planning our worship in such a way as to make the dimension of mission as explicit as possible. Worship is creative of Christian *community* because it is the activity of God who calls whom he wills and incorporates them within the one Body. That does not mean that *we* do not have to think out ways in which our worship may best express our Christian fellowship and extend and deepen it through its words and actions and through the formative effect these words and actions have on our characters. Indeed, it means we have to think out these ways most carefully, and assess how far they are saying and doing what we think they are—for (as we shall also see) there are symbolisms within worship, and the unplanned and undesired symbols may speak louder than those which we consciously contrive.

The paradox of worship is the paradox of grace. If we try to repress one side of that paradox, then our understanding of worship will be lopsided and maimed. Though it is God who worships within us, we are not absolved from working out our own worship with fear and trembling. The cosinesses of Quietism are not compatible with the paradox of worship.

Nor, however, are the excesses of activism. We need both intellect and imagination to plan a worthy act of worship, but the work and effort we put into it are not unaided human work and effort. We could not even desire God if he had not already put it into our heart to do so. We cannot therefore congratulate ourselves on ascribing due worth to God, and imagine how gratified he must feel at the honours we are heaping upon him; our very worship is a response to his initiative, and a response—moreover—that we could not even begin to make or desire if it were not for God himself working within us, in our responding, enabling us both to desire and to do.

Let us now see how the paradox of grace illuminates our understanding of what is happening in the various aspects of our worship. For instance, when we adore, does our worship affect simply ourselves, or does our adoration do anything to God? Our first reaction is to say that its effect is simply an effect on ourselves. God cannot possibly be enhanced by anything *we* do—infinity plus anything still equals infinity. 'My soul doth magnify the Lord', we sing, and immediately want to qualify the statement. We do not and cannot magnify the Lord, we say—any more than a magnifying glass magnifies the print on the page. All it does is to make the print appear larger to our eyes, so that we can read what would otherwise appear too tiny to distinguish. The effect is not on the page, but on our apprehension of the page. Is this not the case also with our apprehension of God as we magnify him in our worship?

> In my heart, though not in heaven,
> I can raise thee.

It *is* the case until we apply to it the *paradox* of adoration. Love has created us, but the very act of creation is a voluntary self-limitation of God in that thenceforth he can only receive love from the human part of his creation if it is freely offered. If men decide not to answer the free love of God by a free and loving response, the Creator is hurt, sorrowful, diminished—whatever we may say about the divine impassibility, whatever we may say about infinity minus anything still being infinity. Conversely, however, if his creation *does* decide to return love for love, the Creator rejoices. The arc of divine love is made into a perfect circle by the answering love of man. God's perfection returns; he is magnified. We have ascribed worth to him, and he has not remained unaffected by our worship. The paradox of worship gives meaning to our adoration and thanksgiving.

Again, it is the paradox of worship (which is the paradox of grace) which enables us to pray for forgiveness. We cannot confess our sins without the rider 'as we forgive those who sin against us'. The rider might make us imagine that divine forgiveness depends upon human attitudes and that therefore it was the human aspect rather than the divine which was determinative; but the paradox of forgiveness—which is the paradox of grace—casts us straight back on to the fact that *we* cannot forgive others unless *God's* reconciling love uses us as its channel. We offer our own forgiveness to others in fear and trembling; but it is God who forgives in us.

Or again, the paradox of grace prevents us from the wrong kind of petitions or intercessions in our worship. We cannot ask selfishly, either for ourselves or for others, when we know that our very asking must be enabled and inspired by the God to whom we direct our petitions, if there is to be any chance of his granting those requests. Only if *he* asks in *our* asking, will he grant our desires.

In all these aspects of prayer and worship, we cannot dispense with either half of the paradox. We cannot assume that worship is all of God, or there would be no need to add our human prayers to God's all-sufficient ones. Nor can we assume that worship is all of man, for that is the ultimate blasphemy which reduces God from an end into the means. The paradox of grace assures us that worship is hard work, requiring human effort and will. It assures it is necessary work, actually achieving something within the divine economy. Yet it reassures us that we would have no will to worship if it were not given us by God, and no effectiveness to our worship had not God designed it so. If it is true that worship is *opus Dei*, we have to remember that the genitive in that phrase is of ambiguous import. It can mean that worship is God's work in the sense that it is the work we do in the service of God. It can mean that worship is God's work in the sense that it is the very activity of God himself. The ambiguity must not be resolved. We must hold both meanings, and hold each firmly and without compromise or weakening, if the creative tension of the paradox of grace is to inform our understanding and our practice of worship.

2

WORSHIP AND
BELIEF

The paradox of worship is that the initiative comes from God, and yet that does not absolve us from the need to give of our utmost in human effort to make the worship as adequate as we are able. To forget either side of the paradox is to have an unbalanced idea of what worship is and what it involves. Thus if we limit our understanding of worship to 'ascribing worth' to God, it becomes an exercise in which human criteria are determinative. The same is true of thinking of worship as a human exploration, a 'groping after' God. If worship is no more than that, we have forgotten that the prodigal's movement of return is a great deal less significant than the fact that the father has run out to meet him. God is present in our very gropings towards him—'thou wouldest not be seeking me if thou hadst not already been found of me'.[1] On the other hand, if we discount the human aspect of worship, and think of worship purely as a divine activity to which we are privileged to listen and in which we may make bold to join, the balance is just as far out on the other side. Perhaps the most adequate single word to do justice to the paradox of worship is the word 'response'—a response which it is our duty to make as adequate as possible to the nature of the God who has made the first move.

Duty? No, that is too cold a word. St Paul felt that he *had* to preach the Gospel, because he had no choice—it would have been misery to him not to preach (1 Cor. 9.16). Jeremiah tried not to call the LORD to mind nor speak in his name, but found that his word was imprisoned in his body like a fire blazing in his heart, so that he was weary with holding it under, and could endure no more (Jer. 20.9). The same is true of the worshipper. Once he has become conscious of the hand of God upon him, there is a divine necessity which brooks no denial. When worship has become the response to the experienced reality of God which a man feels as a divine compulsion within his bones, then the call to worship has that inner driving force which cannot be denied. A man feels he has to worship or burst.

As soon as Jacob has seen the ladder full of angels going up and down between heaven and earth, there is no need to cajole or bribe him into worship. It would take more than persuasion to *stop* him from setting up his altar and sacrificing. When Paul and Silas (Acts 16.19–34) have been flung into a filthy, stinking gaol where the riff-raff and rag-tag of the town have been thrown overnight to cool off, they sing their hymns of praise to God in the middle of the night to the inconvenience of their fellow-prisoners and the astonishment of their gaoler. It would be hard to imagine a more off-putting set of circumstances for worship. The pews were uncomfortable, the time inconvenient, the company uncongenial. There were no liturgical trimmings or advertising gimmicks to persuade Paul and Silas to come to worship. That mattered not the least. They knew themselves to have been taken hold of by the Holy Spirit and they knew that God was doing great things with them. In such a situation, worship was inevitable. There was no stopping them.

Or again, there was no need of a visiting preacher and massed choirs to persuade those persecuted Christians of the pre-Constantinian Church to turn out of bed before dawn on a Sunday morning and to pad through the deserted streets to their meeting-place where they were going to break bread together before beginning the work of the day. That twenty-minute service at half-past four or five o'clock in the morning was brief and ordinary and unassuming and outwardly unexciting, but there was something about it which made men risk home, liberty, even life itself, to take part in it. As Gregory Dix reminded us, it

was homely and unemotional to a degree. The christian came to the eucharist ... not to seek a psychological thrill. He came simply to *do* something, which he conceived he had an overwhelming personal duty to do, come what might. What brought him to the eucharist week by week, despite all dangers and inconveniences, was no thrill provoked by the service itself, which was bare and unimpressive to the point of dullness, and would soon lose any attraction of novelty. . . . What brought him was an intense belief that in the eucharistic action of the Body of Christ, as in no other way, he himself took a part in that act of sacrificial obedience to the will of God which was consummated on Calvary and which had redeemed the world, including himself.[2]

There was no need of gimmickry or psychological bribery to get a Christian to worship; you could not drag him away from it by the threat of wild lions.

The tragedy with worship is when this is no longer true, and worship has become a dull bore. There are many places where the visitor feels that the life has gone out of a congregation. It seems as if the people are continuing to come only out of habit, not out of conviction. Yet they cannot have altogether given up believing; if they had, they would have deserted the Church altogether. Maybe they are like the people of whom the sociologist Peter Berger writes: they have heard 'a rumour of angels'. It could be a false rumour; but what if it were true? It is in the hope that it may be true that the worshippers hang on to an observance which almost belies the rumour which sustains it. The problem of worship today is part of a much deeper problem—the problem of the tentativeness of so much belief. People do not find it easy to believe; certainly not easy to believe with the robustness which characterized earlier ages in which belief and infidelity were more sharply polarized. Nor do they find it easy to *feel* so strongly about belief. Perhaps that is why they do not find it easy to *feel* about worship. At all events, it is at this deeper level—the level of belief—that we need to concentrate if we are concerned about the deadness of services.

If our worship is dull, it is not because of any lack of showmanship on the part of the clergyman or of musical virtuosity on the part of the organist or the choir, but because the participants (and perhaps even the leader?) have lost their sense of being swept up into the living purposes of an almighty God. We do not renew our worship by brightening up the presentation so that it dazzles by its very entertainment value. We have to go deep; to the hidden springs of worship in the beliefs of the worshipper. It is these hidden springs which we need to feed if the river is ever to flow full and sweet once more. People will find joy and meaning in worship when they feel themselves compelled to respond to the God whom they have begun to apprehend, the God who has begun to reveal himself to them. There will then be a degree of natural inevitability to it. In the words of Mark Gibbard, commenting on the worship of the community at Taizé, they will come to

> feel—and feel increasingly—that they are not so much making an effort as somehow responding, responding to a mysterious reality beyond their grasp, responding to God. They sense that this suits their human nature—that they were made for this.[3]

— ▶▼◀ —

If it is true that worship only becomes real when it is a knowing response to what has been consciously apprehended of the divine, it is also true that the worship which is then offered will mirror a man's understanding of the deity he has perceived. Worship and theology, cult and belief, are inextricably intertwined. It is that connection we now go on to examine.

If a man believes in an angry God who needs to be placated by blood-sacrifices, he will worship in *one* way. If he believes in an irrational God who wants men to throw away their reason and go off into wild and corybantic orgies, he will worship in *another* way. If he is a Christian who believes in a God who has made man's mind and spirit and body, he will worship in a way which uses bodily actions in order to bring about spiritual results, but which does not insult the mind as it does so. His worship will mirror his theology. Leslie Houlden writes that

> Christian worship is not simply a channel of religious feeling or an inroad to the mystery of God. It is an approach by thinking men to a God about whom beliefs are held and who has made it possible for men to speak about him in intelligible terms.[4]

Worship is our response to what God reveals to us of himself. That is why the study of the history of liturgy can be so fascinating; it shows the different ways in which men, through the ages and across the continents, have understood and reacted to their apprehension of (or apprehension *by*) the divine. The task of liturgy is, to quote Leslie Houlden once more, 'to reflect the best understanding of God in the Church of the present'.[5]

It should be obvious that worship and doctrine belong together, but people are not always consistent. Let us look at an example, where tension lies not far below the surface.

Not many people would defend a theology which fences the realm of the sacred off from the realm of the secular and tries to keep lay people away from holy things. Yet that theology is loudly proclaimed in so many of our church services. The holy table is kept from the people by an altar-rail. Beyond it, only the priest may venture; or, at most, an acolyte dressed in quasi-clerical garb. The intention is the laudable one of asserting God's transcendence and of preserving the altar as the numinous area—Mircea Eliade's 'sacred space'—where things beyond our worldly understanding take place; a spot for reverent awe, not to be lightly, unadvisedly, or wantonly trampled upon. But that is not how it comes across. It comes across to the laity as the doctrine that certain spots are too holy for lay feet to walk on—and, conversely, that others are too secular for the clergy to be seen there. I shall never forget a certain New Year's Eve over thirty years ago when I was a choirboy. I was sent from the vestry to the belfry at about 11.40 p.m. with instructions to the bellringer in the tower at the west end of the church that the Vicar wanted to do things differently that year from the way in which they had been done before. The bells were tubular ones, rung from a frame by a single person, and that person was somewhat the worse for wear after his New Year's Eve celebrations. He stood swaying slightly as I gave him the new instructions, but it was obvious even to me that he was in no fit state to take them in, so I repeated them. Then, with slightly slurred speech and slow deliberation, he pronounced his ultimatum. 'Go and tell the Vicar', he said, 'to look after his bloody end of the church, and I'll look after mine'.

That—if we can dignify it with the name—is a theology; but it is a theology of disengagement between the Church (seen in the person of the Vicar) and the secular world. Each has its own proper sphere of activity, and the demarcation must be properly observed. The logical counterpart of that attitude within worship is easily recognized. For religious purposes we use things which are as little like their secular counterparts as possible, lest the worshippers get the idea that there may be any connection between the worship of the sanctuary and the profane world outside. Some things are religious, like gothic script. Others are not, like psychedelic posters. Some things symbolize the divine, like the sound of a mighty organ. Others cannot, like Top of the Pops. If we use bread and wine in a religious context, the wine must not come from the off-licence—it must be fermented grape juice 'shipped under ecclesiastical certificate' and obtained from special suppliers; and the other element must come in the form of peculiar flat white discs that are as unlike everyday bread as can possibly be imagined.

The differences are maintained in an attempt to symbolize the fact that the Church does not capitulate to the world, and that there is something distinctive in a Christian life-style. The message which is perceived is quite different. Would it not be far better to admit common things into sacred worship? That would leave us open to develop the paradox of worship, a paradox in which things can be holy and common at the same time, in which the Holy Communion can show us the latent holiness of the common things of life, in which the world can be seen as charged with the grandeur of God, ready to flame out like shining from shook foil. Jacob's ladder can then be pitched 'twixt Heaven and Charing Cross, and worship will not isolate Christians from the wicked world, but send them back into that world to do something about its wickedness. 'I pray thee, not to take them out of the world, but to keep them from the evil one' (John 17.15).

We must maintain the tension between world-affirming and world-denying within Christian thought (and therefore within Christian worship) as a creative paradox, and not allow it to slip into impotence by repressing one pole of it. The same is true of the rather similar paradoxical tension between the inward-directed and the outward-directed. Is our worship to be directed towards our engagement with the world in the way of mission, or towards our individual relationship to other believers and our inner fellowship with God? Is the purpose of our worship to draw us out of the contaminating world into the contemplation of eternal verities? Or to empower us to go out into the world and change it? In a speech which she made at the New Delhi Assembly of the World Council of Churches in 1961, Mollie Batten seemed to be opting unequivocally for the latter.

> The local church [she said] should fill the role of a supply depot for parachutists rather than an ark for safety. It must never be seen as a social club, or a sphere of continuing activity—*even worship*. It must be a place for the laity to call in for their briefing, for their work in the world; for the sacraments through which they will be cleaned and refitted for duty; for the prayers in which they will lay before God their concerns, and receive new light for their witness, which should be the faithful carrying out of their responsibilities in the structures of the world.[6]

In a comment on that speech, Eric James says that Miss Batten is not here denying the priority of worship. What she is doing is speaking of the nature of the worship of the God who is the redeemer of the *world*. I agree, but I believe that this quotation gives an unduly activist flavour to the whole process of worship, and empties the paradox of its creative tension. Canon James is more aware of the tension than Mollie Batten; he writes that

> Our liturgical action must help us to see the everyday world transformed: the world of industry, commerce, homes, politics local and national, and so on. Worship may take us out of the world *for a time*. Jesus often went apart from the world for a time, for prayer and peace. But he went apart with the very intention of returning to the attack with renewed strength and vigour.[7]

Worship must retain the paradox and the tension. Otherwise it will either become introverted and locked away from the realities of the world, or else so activist that it has no time to drink from the inner springs of renewal and refreshment, or to ask any of the ultimate questions about the purpose of its own activities.

If we go much further with this topic, we shall be straying into the subject of our chapter on worship and mission. Since all we wish to do at present is to highlight the link between worship and belief, let us now take up another example. In terms of worship it will take us into the subject of the chapter on worship and community. In terms of theology it will take us into the relations between transcendence and immanence. In both we shall soon discover that constant sense of paradox which never lies far beneath the surface either of theology or of worship.

The propagandists of the Parish Communion movement within the Church of England have for a long time now been stressing what they believe are the irreconcilable differences between two kinds of setting for the Holy Communion service. The one which they don't like is the 'eight o'clock', where—so they claim—the worshipper comes along to the quiet of the early morning service, creeps into a corner, squats immobile while it all goes on at the other end of the building, and does not get disturbed by the presence of any other member of the congregation:

> You in your small corner
> And I in mine.

His attitude may be exemplified by two parodies of prayer—'Lord, Thou knowest I am on the side of the angels, but don't ask me to worship with them', and 'Bless all natives in foreign parts, and keep them there'.[8] The early morning service, so they tell us, is the liturgical counterpart of an individualist theology—a theology which sees the purpose of God as that of plucking individual brands out of the burning, of saving selected souls out of the miseries of this sinful world and bringing them one by one to a state of solitary contemplation of his glory. It is symbolized in a service held for a handful of self-encapsulated worshippers in a church building from which all sight and sound of this godless generation are excluded.

We are invited to view this theology with revulsion and to feel guilty every time we enjoy the peace and quiet of the early service, because the theology and the worship of the Parish Communion enthusiasts is different. It is a theology of community and a worship which corresponds. God, they say, made the world and enjoys it and likes people who enjoy it; he is interested in company and families and societies and nations. The Church, therefore, they tell us, should not be individualistic like the early morning worshippers. It should worship as a family, a community, a fellowship, young and old together. Each will get into the other's hair at times, but that happens in every family. The babies *will* cry, the kids *will* kick the pews and drop their collection money, and go rummaging noisily around to try and retrieve it, the Youth Club *will* sit in the back pews and giggle, the older members *will* be staid and prefer their way of doing things. But young and old will learn together and be together and worship together and discover that God cares about what they care about.

That, at all events, is the theory. It certainly illustrates that a congregation's doctrine and its style of worship belong together; but I wonder whether the polarities are not too starkly drawn, and whether a truer theology, and therefore a truer style of worship, does not need a dose of paradox or tension? The Parish Communion movement may have been overstressing one side and not allowing the paradox of worship to deepen our understanding of what we are about.

There *is* spiritual value to be found in an early morning celebration, and there *are* dangers in the uncritical espousing of the Family Communion. Geoffrey Fisher was pointing this out to Henry de Candole as long ago as 1939—'As individualism has become a tyranny, so corporateness may become a tyranny'.[9] The quiet early celebration keeps alive that meditative element in worship which is today so desperately needed and which is so often in danger of being crowded out. Silence, solitude, withdrawal—all have their legitimate place within Christian spirituality. To say that 'you can only worship in bedlam' is manifestly absurd; yet bedlam is what the Family Communion can too easily degenerate into, and when it has been made the only fare offered to Sunday morning worshippers, one can sympathize with those who prefer to stay away rather than to be overrun by a horde of uncontrolled children who completely destroy any sense of reverence or any chance of profiting from the readings or sermon. Let us welcome the children, but let them not dominate our worship. There is room for more than one act of parish worship on a Sunday, and it is a doctrinaire mistake to believe that a multiplication of services is destructive of Christian community. As Michael Ramsey was insisting twenty years ago,

> Christian fellowship does not mean getting all the people on to one spot at one hour of the day. It means bringing them into

participation in our Lord (*koinonoi Christou, participes Christi*), in his broken body. It is by participation in *him* that we have our deepest togetherness with one another. I think it is a mistake to exaggerate the place of the physical togetherness of a congregation. If you have one celebration of Holy Communion at 9 and suppress the services at 7 and 8 so that *all* the people are present at 9, is there necessarily more 'fellowship' in the Christian sense? I doubt it.[10]

The early celebration concentrates on the God who is transcendent, beyond our seeing and speaking and imagining; the Family Communion concentrates on the immanence of the God who came into the world of jostling humanity and was edged out onto a Cross between screaming thieves and above dicing soldiers. Neither by itself is a complete response to all we know of God. They must be held together in paradoxical tension, for if either is lost, our faith would be impoverished. Without the leaven of transcendence, the Family Eucharist turns Christian fellowship into mere getting-together, a 'ritual expression of the love which is already present and being exercised within the congregation',[11] indistinguishable from Pelagianism and irreconcilable with the spirituality which finds value in devotion before the Blessed Sacrament. Conversely, without the counterbalance of a sense of immanence, the early celebration becomes unrelated to the real task of a real Church in a real world. The fullness of the faith is only preserved if we allow both to coexist, so that they together bear witness to a religion of paradox. It reminds me of a children's comic my son had some years ago. It came with a pair of spectacles, of which one glass was red and the other green. By closing one eye or the other you got a perfectly conventional flat picture of Jeremy Bear—all very well, but a trifle unexciting. If, however, you kept both eyes open, Jeremy jumped out of the page in living 3-D and his adventures (quite literally) took on another dimension. You had to take two pictures and hold them in one stereoscopic vision if you wanted to have a rounded picture of Jeremy. That is not a bad analogy for what we must do in our worship and our theology if we are to explore the paradox between transcendence and immanence. Its separate terms are at first glance irreconcilable, but it is only if they are both held inviolate that they merge (by some stereoscopic alchemy) into a full, living, and three-dimensional faith by the side of which transcendence by itself or immanence by itself will be seen to be flat, lifeless, and lacking in credibility and appeal.[12]

Our final example of the relationship between worship and belief is the most fundamental. It is that, since Christianity is a sacramental religion, its worship should be based on sacramental principles. This statement should not be taken too narrowly. It does not refer only (nor indeed primarily) to the Eucharist. A sacrament is an 'outward and visible sign of an inward and spiritual grace', and it is needed because man is body as well as spirit. If a man's spirit is moved, then his body has to do something in order both to express and to effect that response to the numinous awareness.

When Jacob arose from his sleep and said 'How fearsome is this place!' (Gen. 28.17), he started *building*. When Paul and Silas in prison in Philippi had sung and prayed, and the miracle had happened, and the gaoler had been half scared out of his wits, he came to the apostles shivering with the numinous fear which is one of the precursors of worship, and said, 'Masters, what must I *do*?' (Acts 16.30). If you were to ask those early Christians what their worship was about, they would talk in terms of *doing* what Jesus had commanded.

Perhaps these examples are too 'religious' for you. The same is true in more secular contexts. Compare your feelings at the end of two concerts. The first is the Albert Hall on the final night of the Proms. Spirits are high, but the promenaders listen to the music with careful attention; and when it is over, there is the release of tension as the streamers are thrown and there is the jostling and the applause and the calls to conductor and soloists and orchestra and choir. The second is a concert in that sort of church where (for some reason or other of supposed reverence that I have never been able to share) it is judged to be lacking in decorum if clapping is allowed. So the exciting music ends, the emotions are keyed up by it, but all the audience is allowed to do is to file out in respectful silence. Something is lacking. The applause would have had the cathartic effect of allowing the aesthetic emotion to defuse, and the audience would have felt satisfied by having made a physical response to the situation.

It is the same with our worship. Worship may be a response to a numinous awareness which far transcends the physical, but unless it is expressed in physical form, by action, in visible symbol, it will only be a partial and unsatisfying response. Liturgy is our answer to what God has disclosed to us of his worshipful activity, and we must needs act out what we discover of him.

This is not always realized. In a recent article in *New Testament Studies* on 'The Eucharist and the Epistle to the Hebrews', the Epistle was examined and it was concluded (correctly, I believe) that it had no explicit references to the Eucharist, although there were places where scholars had previously thought they could detect echoes of a familiarity with the sacrament. Where the author (in my submission) went beyond the evidence and off the rails was when he used the data of the Epistle to the Hebrews to reach such conclusions as

> By faith . . . the worshipper has direct access to the throne of grace, with no need of physical mediation of a sacramental, cultic kind. . . . One of the distinctive emphases of Hebrews may well be a view, not shared by other New Testament writers, that the sacrifice of Christ was of a kind that rendered obsolete every form of cultus that placed a material means of sacramental communion between God and the worshipper.[13]

That not only goes far beyond the evidence by arguing too eloquently from silence; it also sets forth a view about Christianity and Christian worship which I believe to be most profoundly untrue. It is a view which crops up from time to time in association with many kinds of heretical (generally Puritanical, Manichee, or Gnostic) theologies. It belongs to that type of rationalism which views the materialization of the spiritual with a sense of incredulous horror. John Kent, for instance, quotes a seventeenth-century Unitarian catechism which stated that the New Covenant was

> altogether spiritual; being placed not in external things which from their nature conduce nothing to virtue, but in things internal, possessing some natural moral value. But external rites, commonly denominated ceremonial, are not spiritual, nor do they

of themselves and from their nature at all conduce to virtue and piety.[14]

We sense the utilitarian view of worship which subordinates it to the inducement of moral virtue and feelings of piety; and we are not surprised that what Dr Kent calls a 'spiritualized cult without a cultus' had no staying power.

A 'spiritualized cult without a cultus' is not the Christian way of worship. Christians worship with the senses as well as with the mind, and are not ashamed to use bread and wine, water, a ring, or the laying on of hands, to express and effect things which go on at the spiritual level. Nor are they ashamed to use music, vestments, liturgical choreography, lights and sounds and smells. All may converge into a truly spiritual act of worship, not in spite of the fact that they are material things, but precisely *because* they are material things. Man's dual nature means that the outward appearance does not exhaust for him the spiritual efficacy of the physical world. The relation between material and spiritual is a paradoxical one; for that very reason it hides great profundities within it.

Our worship is intimately linked with what we believe. It is not surprising, therefore, that an era of theological ferment is also a time of liturgical change. What principles should guide us as we try to revise our liturgies and renew our worship in days when the very bases of theology are being so widely and so radically questioned?

We need to revise our liturgy in order the better to express through it the beliefs of the Church in the idiom of the worshippers. Note that it is the *Church's* beliefs, not those of the individual members of the congregation: and it is the *worshippers'* idiom, not that of any other person or group. Let us look a little more closely at both these points.

Liturgy should express the Church's beliefs. A service of worship presupposes commitment. The worshippers are not, however, necessarily committed to a particular and dogmatic corpus of beliefs, but they *are* committed to a body of people which is the heir to and trustee of those beliefs. (They are also, if the worship is Christian worship, committed to a Person who is the truth; but we will let that by for the moment.) Our individual grasp of Christian truth may well be tentative, hesitant, or even defective; but we belong to the Church because we think it worth while to make a spiritual pilgrimage along tracks which our forebears in the Church have charted. Our worship is intended for those who are committed to the search for truth within the Christian community. It ought to help them to express, in as direct and unambiguous a way as possible, the historic beliefs of that community, the things which mark it off from the world and from those who see truth in different guise. That is the way of honesty. The Church must be honest about the nature of its own faith, and those who join with its company can then be honest about their own feelings or lack of feelings, and about the mental and spiritual reservations which they as individuals have about that faith. But the worship must express the corporate faith, not the individual reservations, or the worshipper will never get any further along his pilgrimage. In any case, since every congregation contains an almost infinite gradation of belief from the frankly agnostic through the wistfully half-believing to the unshakeably convinced, the only practical thing to do is to make the worship mirror standard doctrine, not individual vagaries.

The idiom in which worship is conducted, however, must be that of the congregation, and not of some other person or group. We should not alter the liturgy in order to woo more effectively those casual half-hearted 'fringe' worshippers who drift into a service without commitment, or to win back the lapsed 'who would', so we fool ourselves into saying, 'come back if only we could brighten up the services a bit'. To quote Geddes MacGregor, 'liturgy is not primarily a means of cajoling people to seek out God; it is, rather, the means of expressing the love that is already in the hearts of those whom God has touched in his own mysterious ways'.[15] It is dishonest to invent a style of worship which is not our own in order to lure into it people who have not had a hand in the ordering of it. These people will—quite rightly—remain unimpressed. It is no good importing the Mersey Sound into the Mass, or doing Rock of Ages to Rock 'n' Roll, or having Benediction with Bagpipes (or whatever the pop cult of the passing moment has on its 'Top Twenty') in the hopes that it will (as the saying goes) 'bring young people into the Church'. The young people themselves will see through the dishonesty of the situation more quickly than their elders. On the other hand, if there are *already* young people who are believing members of the congregation, whose conviction it is that God can be rightly worshipped in this idiom, and for whom this idiom is a natural means of expression, then *for them* it is right so to worship—as their own offering to God of their own natural worship, not as evangelism disguised as entertainment. The same goes for the idioms of worship within a multiracial or multicultural society; in the immigrant areas of Britain, for example, or between Maori and Pakeha in New Zealand. And, since the congregation is a family, a fellowship, it is right that the other members of the family should let the minority have its head on occasion. But only on occasion, because no member of the family, young or old, trad or square, brown or white, has the right to force his own particular mode of worship on the whole of the congregation all the time.

If our worship is successful in that primary purpose of expressing the Church's faith in the congregation's idiom, then it may have that extra, unplanned bonus which happens when the outsider or the lapsed comes into the service and discovers that there is something about it and about the congregation which is offering it, something which makes him want to know in greater detail what it is all about. The service was not designed with him in mind, but nonetheless it seems to be drawing him. The Lord is adding day by day to their number those whom he is saving, and he is able to do it because the worship which is being offered is relevant to the community which offers it.

What goes for the idioms of the presentation of worship also goes for the thought-forms within which that worship is expressed. They too must be such as to 'ring bells' with the community which is taking part in the act of worship. Unfortunately, though they have gone some way towards this, so many of our new liturgies do not seem to have done it either with sufficient determination or at sufficient depth. There has been modernization of the language, but translation needs to be more than purely verbal if the rite is to have the same impact for the people of our day as it had for our ancestors. We need to apply new theological insights to the material of the rite, and we need to have a very careful eye to its imagery and symbolism.

In theology, there has been some change in emphasis—for example, the studious removal from the new eucharistic rite of the Church of England of the concept of a 'moment of consecration', and the playing-down of the Passion aspect in favour of an *anamnesis* of the whole range of the mighty acts of the Lord from creation to consummation. There are theologians, however, who believe this has done no more than toy with the real issues. Leslie Houlden claims that the Church of England's most recent eucharistic rite is still

> archaic. . . . Apart from a few traces of Reformation emphases (more now than in Series 2), there is little sign of any development in Christian theology since patristic times, let alone in the last hundred years.[16]

The example he takes is the way in which the Thanksgiving Prayer talks about *acts* of God as though creation and redemption are past history rather than continuing and living realities.

What is equally serious (and worth spending a little time discussing) is the way in which the imagery of the new rites so often retains old symbolisms which no longer have currency for the worshippers who have to use them. To take a blatant example, in the Thanksgiving Prayer of Series 3

> we praise God for creation through Jesus, his living Word. We appeal thereby to a biblical and patristic concept, that of Christ as the pre-existent Logos, which is more remote from present-day thought than almost any other and which is so far removed from readily accessible imagery that its evocative power is minimal, except for the initiated. Hardly one worshipper in thousands can be expected to find it an appropriate expression of his faith.[17]

'Logos' is not the only alien symbol in our revised liturgies. The symbol of the sacrificial lamb, for instance, highly relevant though it may have been for Biblical society, needs careful explanatory teaching before it can mean a thing to present-day Westerners—even to those still living in an agricultural milieu.

The image of God as King speaks more readily to a monarchical than to a republican society, and even there, the nature of monarchy has so changed over the ages that the symbol can mislead as easily as it may illuminate. It is intended to speak of God's majesty and transcendence, and of his concern for everything that goes on in the whole earth. Its meaning is that religion is no peripheral or sectional concern, because God, like the monarch, is 'in *all* causes, as well ecclesiastical as temporal, supreme'. This is no longer the kind of power exercised by a present-day monarch. It is not even true of the monarch-in-Parliament, for Parliament today has to compete for authority with increasingly powerful Trades Unions and multi-national corporations—to say nothing of the European Economic Community. Therefore, because kingship is no longer experienced as a total bond between monarch and nation, as the centre of a complex web of rights and duties applying to both king and people, the God to whom this symbol is referred becomes misunderstood—either in terms of the king of an unreal fairy-story, or as the remote artificer of the Deists, or as an arbitrary and tyrannical despot. The symbol has become more of an embarrassment than an illumination.

Symbols like lambs and thrones and altars, which are closely related to a particular economic, political, and cultic structure, easily become obsolete when retained within a society different from the one in which they came to birth.

If we retain symbols after they have ceased to be centrally related to our society there will not only be loss of communication, but there is also the danger of a serious distortion of our vision of God.[18]

What then should we do? Change the symbols for new and more up-to-date ones? That is what a recent writer in *Theology*[19] wishes us to attempt. Easier said than done. New symbols do not arise easily, and if we try to manufacture them rather than wait for them to well up naturally, we are worse off than we were before. To jettison the symbol of monarchy and to speak of the Great Trades Union Secretary in the Sky tells us, by its very risibility, that we are a hundred miles from success. God as The Great Mathematician seems to have had a limited currency, but not so much has been heard of this image recently. The only recent new symbol which I can bring to mind which has even the remotest chance of 'sticking' is the symbol used of Christ in the musical *Godspell*: the symbol of the clown.

The clown is the man who stands apart from society, who is regarded as cracked and crazy and who may therefore say what he wants without danger of contradiction. The disconcerting thing about him is that what he says is so often a shrewd comment which gets to the heart of the matter. Christ is the court jester, the fool, the odd man out—yet behind his rash paradoxes and his overdrawn hyperboles, there is the most profound truth which we laugh away at our peril.

I mentioned this symbol of the clown as a new one. It is not, of course. It was used of the prophets of old (2 Kings 9.11, Jer. 29.26, Hos. 9.7), and Paul used it of Christians in 1 Corinthians 3.18. Perhaps it is not even any longer a current symbol. Court jesters are as obsolete as courts, and even the circus is becoming a less familiar sight except on television on Christmas Day. Yet the cartoonist continues the tradition of the clown; he gets us to drop our defences with a wry smile, and laughs us into recognizing the truth.

But *is* the solution to our difficulty to be found in the abandoning of obsolete symbols and the minting of new ones? A more satisfactory solution would be to realize that symbols, like analogies, can only take us so far. Ultimately they break in our hands. The better the symbol and the closer it is to the reality to which it points us, the further we shall be able to take it before it *does* break. But break it will, for it is only a symbol and not the very truth himself. When we speak of obsolescent or obsolete symbols, we mean symbols which break earlier today than they did in former civilizations. They can still be used, but they are nothing like so serviceable as they once were. When they are used (and used they will be, for they still have an evocative power, perhaps through their very antiquity and the way in which they seem to pluck the chords of what Jung used to call the 'collective unconscious') they have to be balanced with their counter-symbols. We need, not fewer symbols, not (necessarily) new symbols, but more symbols. That way, no one symbol will ever be in danger of being mistaken for 'the truth, the whole truth, and nothing but the truth'. If we are confronted in our worship with a riot, a plethora, a profusion of symbols, then each will be able to correct its neighbour and through the kaleidoscope of imagery we may be able to catch a glimpse of the sacred and ineffable reality which lies behind all our shifting and partial expressions.

> Jesus! My Shepherd, Husband, Friend,
> My Prophet, Priest, and King,
> My Lord, my Life, my Way, my End,
> Accept the praise I bring.[20]

That tenfold symbolism in a verse from an eighteenth-century hymnologist is a pointer to us. It was what Ian Ramsey was after when he spoke to us of models and qualifiers and the need to range freely over a wide variety of symbols in our discourse about God.[21] We will have to do the same if we want our worship and our belief to cohere in these present days of theological upheaval.

The renewal of worship calls for no superficial thinking in days when belief and the way in which belief is expressed are changing in such a bewildering way. Any attempts to renew, or freshen up, or revise, or update our worship without close attention to theological factors and their relation to the convictions and natural idioms of the worshippers, are mere gimmickry. And a gimmick is a bright idea designed to draw in the crowds without first thinking what it is they are being drawn in to, and without considering whether the bright idea is saying the right things. When we have that, we deceive ourselves into thinking we are achieving renewal whilst we are only having novelty.

There is a fundamental difference between renewal and novelty. The Athenians, you will remember, 'and the foreigners there had no time for anything but talking or hearing about the latest novelty' (Acts 17.21). The pursuit of novelty is the continual striving after effect, the constant struggle to be newer than tomorrow, the never-ending attempt to wake up a jaded palate, and to shout louder and louder so that those who are not deafened will hear you. With novelty, we get a steadily-decreasing reaction to a steadily-increasing stimulus, and the effort is ultimately self-defeating. When the Seer of the Book of the Revelation hears Jesus say, 'Behold! I am making all things new!' (Rev. 21.5), this is not what he understands. Renewal is seeing 'the dearest *freshness* deep down things',[22] being able to look at the dawn as though one had never seen the sun rise before, experiencing what J. V. Taylor has called 'the flashes of sudden recognition, of seeing the ordinary in an extraordinary way, which the Holy Spirit gives to every man'.[23] Renewal is not novelty, it is freshness. We will renew our liturgy by seeing it with fresh eyes, understanding it as we had not understood it before, seeing what we are doing and why we are doing it, and using our understanding to penetrate to the inner springs of the creative liturgy of God himself.

When we embark on this, we generally find that there are changes which we want to make in the way in which we express our worship, in order the better to embody what it is we discover about God. The question now is, what kind of changes are legitimate?

A parable based on an incident in the Old Testament may not be out of place here. When King David was bringing the Ark of the Covenant from its temporary resting-place in the house of Abinadab to its permanent home in Jerusalem, we read (2 Sam. 6.3) that 'they mounted the Ark of God on a new cart'. The Ark had got stuck. It could not move. There was nothing doing. It was only when the Ark was lifted up and put upon a new cart that the next stage in the pilgrim history of the People of God could get under way. We find this happening in the midst of dancing and singing and rejoicing: 'David and all Israel danced for joy before the LORD without restraint to the sound of singing, of harps and lutes, of tambourines and castanets and cymbals' (2 Sam. 6.5).

The Ark itself contained the holy things—the two tablets of God's holy Law, the pot of manna, and Aaron's rod that budded. These things took Israel back to the moment when a rabble of slaves was called out by God and turned into his chosen nation. They were to be the centre of Israelite religion, not subject to change. The Ark could not be made new; but the superstructure, the things around it, the paraphernalia, the cart which carried the Ark—this could be replaced. Indeed, if the Ark were to be where God wanted it to be, there *had* to be a new cart. And Uzzah and Ahio, sons of Abinadab, could guide the new cart and be commended for doing so. But 'when they came to a certain threshing-floor, the oxen stumbled, and Uzzah reached out to the Ark of God and took hold of it. The LORD was angry with Uzzah and struck him down there for his rash act. So he died there beside the Ark of God' (2 Sam. 6.6).

There, in that primitive piece of Old Testament superstition, we may read a parable. True, the original significance of the newness of the cart was a purely ritual one; true, the offence of Uzzah was in origin that of a ritually unclean touch on the purity of God's possessions; but it is legitimate to see the incident in allegorical terms. The men of Israel could fiddle with the cart as much as they liked, but let Uzzah put forth his hand and try to steady the Ark itself; let him assume that God could not look after himself, but that he needed human help to be going on with, and he was struck down for his rashness. The Ark—the central truths of our faith—is not subject to change, and woe betide the man who thinks it is and tries to interfere. Renewal of worship cannot come about by fiddling with the essentials or trying to accommodate the central truths of the faith to what we think people will swallow. It is no good trying to water down the faith so that people can be offered something that they can swallow without difficulty. By the time it is watered down, it becomes so tasteless that it is not worth swallowing. Dean Inge half a century ago warned us that the man who marries the Spirit of Today will be a widower tomorrow. Reductionism has no future. The churches on the move, the churches where things are happening, the churches which know what 'renewal' means, are those which are resting on the great central and eternal affirmations of the Christian faith—Jesus the Son of God, the Holy Spirit the power of God, prayer as a force in the lives of people who give themselves over to the free service of Almighty God. Here are people whose Ark is stable, who reckon with 'Jesus Christ . . . the same yesterday, today, and for ever' (Heb. 13.8).

The Ark must not change. It needs a new cart. It is part of today's travail to distinguish between the Ark which cannot and must not be changed and the cart which can and which must be made new. In our organization, our ministry, our theological formulations, our understanding of the Bible, we have to tell what is cart and what is Ark, and renew the one whilst not interfering with the other. The same is true of our worship and its relations with our understanding of the faith. It will not be an easy task; the success with which it is done will have immense bearing on the shape of the Church of the next generation.

3

WORSHIP AND
COMMUNITY

Christian worship is a paradox. There are two directions in which we have been trying to understand it—as a human activity directed towards God, or as God's activity into which we may enter. We have discovered that if we try to think of worship in terms of either of these directions to the exclusion of the other, we lose our balance. God's initiative does not make human effort unnecessary: man's effort does not imply that God has nothing to do but sit back and accept our offering. Worship is an encounter between man and God in which any attempt to make a rigid separation between the two parties and their contribution to the total act is fatal.

So far we have seen this paradox in terms of what we might call the vertical dimension—in terms of relations between man and God. In the next two chapters we intend to explore it in horizontal terms—that is, in terms of relationships between human beings. We shall, however, try to use the words 'horizontal' and 'vertical' as little as possible, partly because their use in this sense has been rather overdone in some recent theological writing, and partly because it does not always lead to felicitous results. For example, I was once sent a booklet for review, on the subject of informal Eucharists, which contained the unfortunate sentence: 'A meal especially emphasizes the horizontal fellowship of the congregation.' The mind boggled.

This present chapter is about 'worship and community'—worship as the activity whereby the Church builds up its fellowship and expresses its community and nature. The next chapter will be on 'worship and mission'. Both these activities could be regarded as horizontal ones—the first inwardly-directed and the second outwardly-facing. It is immediately obvious that we are once again faced with paradox. If we try to understand the horizontal without the vertical, or the inward-directed without the outward-facing, we shall be in trouble.

Worship is like a rope which consists of a threefold strand. Community, theology and mission—the inward, the upward, and the outward—are inseparable and inextricable. If we try to understand any one of them without taking the other two into account, we shall be lost. The way in which they form a single rope is obvious in the text we have already quoted once before, from Acts 2.41–7: 'Those who accepted [Peter's] word'—those, that is, who had been touched and converted, and who wanted to enter a new relationship with God in Christ; those who had accepted a certain set of beliefs—'were baptized, and some three thousand were added to their number that day. They met constantly to hear the apostles teach, and to share the common life, to break bread, and to pray.' The theology, the upward dimension, led to community, a sharing in the common life, which was instanced in the breaking of bread and the praying—the worship. 'And', we read, 'day by day the Lord added to their number those whom he was saving'—the mission of God was inextricably linked with the community and the theology.

Although in this chapter we shall be concentrating on the relationship between worship and community, we must bear in mind that it is only a partial picture we are painting; otherwise we shall fall into the trap of planning the sort of worship which will lead Christians into narcissistic self-regard instead of taking their part in the paradox whereby God builds up his outward-facing, missionary community.

Thus: To think of worship and community without *mission* is to deal with a cosily introverted in-group subject. God is a God of mission, and the community he calls out is called out, not for a self-regarding purpose, but in order to share and to help make more effective that mission of God to his whole creation.

To think of worship and mission without *community* is to make Christianity an individualistic affair—which is as near a contradiction in terms as we can get.

To think of *mission* without the vertical dimension is to pervert it into an attempt to win people over to your own opinions rather than to share with others the good news of what God has done in Jesus and is continuing to do through the Holy Spirit.

To think of *community* without grounding our treatment of the subject within the vertical dimension is even more disastrous. If our understanding of it is limited to the horizontal dimension, 'community' tells us how a group of likeminded people can cohere; and there is nothing particularly significant about *that*. Any group of likeminded people find that if they share a common external interest, this interest binds the group together—whether that interest be flower arranging, rugby football, railway preservation, or political ideology. Cohering is not worshipping. Cohering is what happens when a group is interested in a subject over which *they* have control. Worshipping is what happens to a group which has been caught hold of by something greater than the group, which takes the initiative and makes the group feel of distinctly secondary importance.

Clearly, there is a spectrum here. Even within the secular sphere, some groups have a relation to their subject which is closer to worship than that of some others. The political cell is nearer to a sense of being controlled and united by an external and over-riding ideological object than is (for example) the cookery class. The Christian is aware of this spectrum, but claims that the relation between him as worshipper and God as the object of his worship is not contained within it. At the most, the spectrum contains a set of 'direction indicators' which can point a man towards understanding the unique divine/human relationship which is worship. The understanding itself comes through what Bishop Ian Ramsey used to call a 'disclosure', congruent with, but not contained within, the series which points to it. That is because, for the Christian, the nature of his community and fellowship is *sui generis*. It is a community called forth, and created, by the transcendent Object towards which its worship is directed.

Once more, paradox is inescapable. We can write (as I did a few paragraphs ago) of 'worship as the activity whereby the Church builds up its fellowship and expresses its community and nature'; yet the Christian knows that it is *God* who chooses *us* (cf. John 15.16), and our Christian fellowship is his body and of his making. Yet what is of God does not thereby cease to depend upon human effort.

Christians work to create their Christian community with fear and trembling, knowing that it is God who creates in them both to will and to do.

— ▶▼◀ —

The people of the Old Testament would have been rather surprised at the thought of anybody discussing 'Worship and Community'. The link between the two would have been thought so obvious that it did not need to be pointed out. We do meet with the worship of the individual in the Old Testament, but the predominant aspect of Israelite worship is that it is the worship of a community. Moreover, that community is not a self-created one, but one which has been called out and made into what it is by Jahveh its God. The people of the Old Testament took over many of the cultic practices of surrounding nations, but they often reinterpreted them in terms of their own community and its covenant-relationship with Jahveh as they did so. Let us take as our example their harvest festival customs.[1]

This nomadic people coming in from the wilderness and taking over the land from its former occupants, would need to learn both the science and the theology of agriculture. The theology was as important as the technology. It was the god of the land who showed them how to sow and tend and harvest the crops he gave them:

> Will the ploughman continually plough for the sowing,
> breaking his ground and harrowing it?
> Does he not, once he has levelled it,
> broadcast the dill and scatter the cummin?
> Does he not plant the wheat in rows
> with barley and spelt along the edge?
> Does not his God instruct him and train him aright?
> Dill is not threshed with a sledge,
> and the cartwheel is not rolled over cummin;
> dill is beaten with a rod,
> and cummin with a flail. . . .
> This message, too, comes from the LORD of Hosts.
>
> (Isa. 28.24–7, 29)

The first stage, therefore, in relating harvest to the worship of the God who sent the harvest, is to link the harvest rites to the seasonal cycle of husbandry. This we find in the earliest strata of the Pentateuch. The J and E harvest rituals in Exodus 23.16 and 34.22 tell the worshipper to

> celebrate the pilgrim-feast of Harvest, with the firstfruits of your work in sowing the land, and the pilgrim-feast of Ingathering at the end of the year, when you bring in the fruits of all your work on the land.

The worshipper is instructed to

> observe the pilgrim-feast of Weeks, the firstfruits of the wheat harvest, and the pilgrim-feast of Ingathering at the turn of the year.

There is a brief reference to the Exodus from Egypt in connection with the Feast of Unleavened Bread in Exodus 23.15 and 34.18, but that is as far as it goes. 'The blood of my sacrifice' is mentioned in 23.18 as never having to be offered at the same time as anything leavened, and to this the parallel passage in 34.25 adds mention of 'the victim of the pilgrim-feast of Passover.'[2] But it is clear that at this early stage, the main thrust of the description shows us an agrarian festival. This is the proper way of celebrating before God the barley and the wheat harvest (which are separated in practice by a period of seven weeks) and the ingathering at the year's end.

By the time we reach the book of Deuteronomy, this seasonal cycle has become related to the historical facts of the calling of the Israelite community by Jahveh. The cycle of feasts is no longer agricultural but community–historical. In Deuteronomy 16.1–17, the whole emphasis has changed. The Festival of Unleavened Bread is not the festival of the barley harvest, but the Passover, 'for it was in that month that the LORD your God brought you out of Egypt by night'. Unleavened bread is eaten because it is 'the bread of affliction' and 'in urgent haste you came out of Egypt'. The victim is slaughtered 'in the evening as the sun goes down, the time of your coming out of Egypt'. Seven weeks later the Feast of Weeks is kept—not primarily because it is the wheat-harvest, but so that 'you shall . . . remember that you were slaves in Egypt'. The Feast of Ingathering, the vine harvest, is now called 'the pilgrim-feast of Tabernacles' and is kept as a community feast by 'your sons and daughters, your male and female slaves, the Levites, aliens, orphans, and widows who live in your settlements'. The feasts have become transformed into ones dominated by the theme of historical memory, thanksgiving, and renewed self-consecration to the Covenant which binds together the community and its God.

Similarly, in Deuteronomy 26, as Dr Robert Murray points out,

the meaning of the action is expressed entirely in terms of historical confession and thanksgiving, in the famous 'creed' beginning 'A wandering Aramaean was my father' (Deut. 26.5). The object is clear: the worshipper is performing an act of worship common to the Canaanites, but is making it abundantly clear that he is thanking not the vegetation god Baal but the historical God of the Fathers, by whose gift the people has been brought into the fertile land of Canaan.[3]

Later still, the Priestly writers develop the idea of the Feast of Weeks being a commemoration of the giving of the Law and the Covenant to God's community, Israel, on Mount Sinai. The P addition at Exodus 19.1 points out that the nation came to Sinai during the season of the Feast of Weeks. The Chronicler shows this Feast as a great liturgical celebration of God's gift of the Law to his community and nation on Mount Sinai. By the time we come to such inter-testamental literature as the Book of Jubilees, the link between the Covenant and the Feast of Weeks has become absolutely explicit:

It is ordained and written on the heavenly tablets, that they should celebrate the feast of weeks in this month once a year, *to renew the covenant every year* (Jubilees 6.17).

Thus it is that we find something as originally pagan and individualist as the barley, wheat, and vine harvests becoming transformed within Israelite worship into the celebration of the birth of God's called-out community and its welding into a holy nation by the Covenant of Sinai when the nation had God's eternal Law, the

Torah, given to it. Part of the genius of the Hebrew people was the way in which it took an agrarian fertility-rite and made it express the truth that God was worshipped in and through a community whom he had created and nurtured through the centuries to be the people of his choice. Worship in ancient Israel took the whole nation, as a nation, back to the moment of its birth. It was an affair between the community and the God who had rescued and created it at the Pasch.

It is not surprising that the same sense of community in worship stayed with the new Israel, the Christian Church. They wished to celebrate their Easter—the new Pasch— the time when the slaying of the Firstborn had redeemed and rescued God's new people (and, through them, in embryo the whole of creation). As the community of the New Israel, they could not imagine a worship where individualism could threaten the life and existence of the community. Or if they could, and were in danger of it, it was because Gentile converts did not have the same basic background understanding of the relation between worship and community.

This is what nearly happened in Corinth. Here we see Paul calling the Church to order before it broke the Body of Christ to pieces by practices which exalted the individual above the community.The very vehemence with which Paul lays about him shows how real the danger was, and how devastating it would have been had the rot not been stopped.

The worship of Christians in Corinth was neither sedate nor pew-bound. It was a meal; and a real meal, not a symbolic sip-and-swallow. There was food enough for all to eat, and wine enough for all to drink. The trouble was that it was not properly shared. Community was thrown overboard because of the greediness and gluttony and winebibbing of individuals who cared more for their own bellies than for the good of the group as a whole. So Paul had to warn them that there were times when their meetings tended to do more harm than good. 'When you meet as a congregation', he thundered,

it is impossible for you to eat the *Lord's* Supper, because each of you is in such a hurry to eat his *own*, and while one goes hungry another has too much to drink. Have you no homes of your own to eat and drink in? Or are you so contemptuous of the church of God that you shame its poorer members? (1 Cor. 11.20–2)

The abuses were regrettable precisely because they separated the well-to-do topers from the poorer members of the congregation who could not afford to bring enough along with them to have quite such a spread. 'I am told', said Paul, and admitted that he believed there was some truth in it, 'that when you meet as a congregation you fall into sharply divided groups' (1 Cor. 11.18). This was no good, because if it was the *Lord's* Supper they were going to eat, they had to *eat* the Lord's body and *be* the Lord's body—and that body could not be divided, as Paul had already insisted (1 Cor. 1.13). (It is, incidentally, interesting to see the way in which Paul begins his letter to Corinth (at 1.13) by a reference to the indivisibility of Christ and then follows that up by playing on the theme of the tripartite meaning of the phrase 'the Lord's body'—in reference to the Eucharist in 1 Corinthians 11, in reference to the Church as the Body of Christ in 1 Corinthians 12, and in relation to the resurrection of the body and Christ's resurrection in 1 Corinthians 15.)

It is not, of course, fortuitous that the Bible shows worship as a community matter; and here we return to the vertical dimension. In worshipping as a community, we are in some way a mirror of the Divinity himself. We are (as the writer to the Hebrews might have said) acting as a parable or shadow or image of God. Christian worship is not a Plotinian flight of the alone to the Alone, but the commerce of a community with God the Holy Trinity. God is not alone; he is community.

In the trinitarian understanding of God [writes Professor J. M. Lochman] the *social character* of the personal God is unmistakably expressed. This can hardly be otherwise in view of the fact that trinitarian theology attempts to consider and witness to the God of biblical history. For the God of biblical history is without doubt the God of his people, the God of men, the God in community. . . . He exists in community. . . . This 'essence' of the biblical God is reflected in the trinitarian doctrine and expressed in terms of God the Father and Son in the community of this Holy

Spirit. The trinitarian doctrine attempts to explain the 'social character' of God. God *means* community, because he *is* community in his essence.[4]

This means that people who relate to this trinitarian God relate not as individuals but in relationships, in communities; and the individual finds his true meaning in the relationship of which he forms a part. Martin Pawley's prophetic book *The Private Future*[5] is a frightening account of the collapse of community, the enthronement of 'privatization', and the dire effects of self-encapsulation on the individual. Pawley is writing entirely of the secular order; Christians have a duty to show how the Church is a community which not only realizes the sickness but provides the cure. 'It is not good for the man to be alone' (Gen. 2.18); but then, neither is God alone. Worship in community answers the needs of man made in the image of God. It is right, both biblically and theologically.

— ▸▾◂ —

We need therefore to ask how our worship may the more thoroughly partake of community nature; how we may express and effect in our worship this togetherness which mirrors the very being of God himself and which was so vivid a feature of the Old and the New Testaments.

Many of the devotional books of an earlier generation taught us to think of worship as a priestly monologue, in which the duty of the people was to follow the words in their prayer books or their confirmation manuals, and to have the right devotional thoughts at the right point in the service. For too long, we Anglicans adopted an attitude of superiority as we castigated the worship of the Roman Catholics (both pre-Reformation and post-Tridentine) for separating the liturgy of the priest from the liturgy of the people and for making the latter no more than receptive passivity—whilst all the time the liturgy of the people in a typical Anglican parish was just as passive as that in any Roman church, and even more prone to individualism and isolationism. Fortunately, that era is dying in both communions, though it is still true that 'the rate of liturgical unemployment [amongst the laity] in contemporary Christendom is staggering'.[6] Old attitudes die hard, and the laity have not been universally pleased to have been rediscovered in the liturgy.

If, however, what we have been saying so far in this chapter has any truth in it at all, the liturgy is a matter for the whole people of God and it is a travesty of liturgy to have a rite which does not need the full co-operation of priest *and* people. We must find ways of ensuring that this theological insight—as much as any of the others which we were discussing in the previous chapters—is written into the rites we use, the way we choose them, and the way in which we convert a written liturgy into speech and action. The liturgy of the people needs to be an active and corporate liturgy, in which the worshippers are built up in the knowledge that they are the body of Christ, called out of the world in order to form God's holy community, and sent back into the world to turn its kingdoms into the Kingdom of God's Christ.

The community which is celebrating the Eucharist is a community greater than that of a single congregation. That is the justification for the set liturgy, in which the unity of a Church spread out over space and through time can be expressed in each individual congregation's act of worship. This brings us to a further paradox within worship; the paradox between structure and freedom, or between formal liturgy and extempore worship.

From time to time there comes the temptation to throw the structured liturgy overboard in favour of something more dependent on the mood of the moment. This temptation is particularly keenly felt in those congregations where a charismatic renewal has established a new and exciting togetherness in the Lord which makes the congregation want to break the bonds of established liturgical structures. The strait-jacket of tradition is compared (unfavourably) with a refreshing and renewing freedom of spirit. It sounds attractive; but it is a dangerous road. The glory of the present charismatic movement (or one of its glories) is that it is taking place within the great historic Churches, challenging them, revitalizing them—and shocking and scandalizing them, too! But in this country at the moment it is not forming new sects and therefore its lessons can be absorbed and its influence felt within the Churches of the mainstream tradition, provided that it does not become the preserve of a tight knot of 'peculiar people'.

If the charismatic movement is to continue and extend its influence, and to be saved from its potential errors and excesses, it must remain within the wider fellowship of the whole Church; and of this wider fellowship, the Church's liturgy is a vital part. A leading charismatic has himself recently written that to be impatient and do things in defiance of Church order

> is to ignore the responsibility that we have as a group to our clergy and congregations. The history of the Church is littered with the sad debris of divisions that have been caused when order has been broken, and a group which decides to 'go it alone' will not be contributing to the glorification of Jesus Christ and the building up of his body.[7]

This is not to say that the worship within a charismatic fellowship is not distinguishable from the worship in its non-charismatic neighbour. Far from it! But it is worship which is framed within the liturgy which that charismatic church shares with its neighbours, which are also parts of the greater communion to which all owe allegiance. What often happens is that charismatic worship is distinguished, not by an abandonment of the set liturgy, but by the addition to it of other elements which have a greater degree of spontaneity to them, elements which express and deepen the sense of community which is growing and developing within the congregation as it discovers afresh the renewing power of possession by God's Holy Spirit. One such addition, known in many charismatic congregations, is the custom of 'singing in the Spirit',

> especially at a eucharist, either as an extension of the *Sanctus* or the doxology in the prayer of thanksgiving, or at the end as an act of praise after Communion.
>
> In this kind of praise each person sings to the Lord in a tongue, or in English, or hums, as the Spirit leads him, and the rest join in spontaneously with a free melody. The sounds blend together in a wonderful harmony. . . . We keep our voices soft so that they do

not dominate the voices of the group, letting the Spirit blend our voice with theirs.[8]

Here, spontaneity does not seem to have created individualism, and the congregation as a whole fellowship is offering this corporate act of songful praise. But this is not the same as creating a new liturgy because the old one is felt to be too staid. The freedom of the Spirit has to accept the constraints which are inescapable within the life of community. The paradox of worship is that structure and freedom can coexist. In the words of Bishop Lesslie Newbigin, 'freedom is not the absence of limits, but the finding and obedient acceptance of the true limit. To be free is to be totally bound to the truth who is Jesus Christ.'[9] God's service (as we are reminded every day at Mattins when we say the Second Collect) is perfect freedom. The original Latin behind that Collect is *cui servire, regnare est*; there is a sovereign freedom in slavery to God. We have the freedom of a monarch within the constraints of a formal order.

It is rather like the freedom of taking part in a performance of a choral work. I remember singing once in the Beethoven *Missa Solennis* (the D major Mass). At first, practices were hard work—sometimes sheer drudgery. Our voices were pushed to the limits of their endurance as the music forced us to maintain an unnaturally high tessitura for bar after bar without remission. ('Gentlemen', said the conductor, 'the first time you sing Bach's B Minor is like your first sight of the Himalayas. The first time you sing Beethoven's Mass in D is like your first attempt to *scale* the Himalayas.') But gradually things began to drop into shape and our tongues and our voice-boxes and our minds got used to the intentions of the composer and we began to *sing*. And, when it all came together, what a glory! The music tumbling out and about (the sheer intricate intoxication of that *et vitam venturi saeculi*); the almost vertiginous sense of dancing on a tight-rope; yet perfectly controlled, rigidly kept in order, in a cascade of sound where one slip would have reduced the whole magical moment to discordant chaos. Yet in it all, the freedom of opening our mouths and our souls to that music which had enslaved us. The same paradox of *cui servire, regnare est* was with us then. John Donne had a glimpse of it in his *Hymne to God my God, in my sicknesse*:

> Since I am coming to that Holy roome,
> Where, with thy Quire of Saints for evermore,
> I shall be made thy Musique. . . .

The choir are the slaves of the music, reigning in sovereign freedom. So are the worshippers as they learn and love the constraints of the liturgy wherein they join as one small part of God's great Church, the community of his saints.

What can we do, in our own churches, to help show forth the truth that worship is a matter of community, and that it is something in which the whole local community of God's people is involved, sharing the liturgy which binds that community to the larger community of the wider Church?

The first thing to note is that the whole Church must be involved in the decision as to which form of worship within the authorized limits shall be used in a church and how that worship shall be staged and presented. If our worship both expresses and constitutes our Christian fellowship, then the ordering of it is the business, not of the priest alone, but of the whole People of God, lay as well as ordained. The involvement of the laity in partnership with the clergy in the planning of the Church's worship is theologically sound. It is also sheer common sense, for people are going to be more committed to worship which they have had a hand in framing than in forms which have been foisted upon them 'from on high'. It is, moreover—at any rate in the Church of England—soundly based in church law. Canon B 3 states that 'decisons as to which of the forms of worship . . . are to be used in any church . . . shall be taken jointly by the minister and the parochial church council', and the Worship and Doctrine Measure of 1974 makes it clear that in the case of a disagreement between the minister and the P.C.C., it is the P.C.C. which has the casting vote.

If worship is worship in the Body of Christ, we need to remember that the local manifestation of that one Body is the unity of pastor and congregation. To work out the worship of a parish as a united body calls for care, prayer, and tact. It is easier in the short run for the priest to adopt the role of the benevolent dictator, as though he were the one man in the whole parish who really knows what is right for it. Partnership, though harder work, is more rewarding. It is only when a congregation has been involved in the understanding and planning of the worship of the parish that that worship begins in a new way to come alive for *them* as *their* worship and not merely as some clerical fad. Otherwise, the clergy of the parish deserve the hard words of the previous Editor of *Theology* when he wrote

> Woe to the shepherds who feed themselves and not the flock; and the clergy *have* fed themselves, indulged their own liturgical addictions to an inordinate degree. For a year or two, they satisfy the more clericalized of their flocks; but the staleness will sicken when surely, and soon, it comes.[10]

The rebuke is well-earned in those parishes where priest and people have not learned and worked together to become at one in their liturgical understanding, their liturgical desires, and their liturgical practice. If the laity have no understanding of the forces behind liturgical change and the reasons for desiring it, and if they are uncomprehending because they are uninvolved, small wonder that in the end they vote with their feet and the congregation dwindles. What is wanted are congregations where priest and people have so worked together at their liturgical understanding that the work of worship is seen by every member of the congregation as a work to be shared, and where decisions about forms of service and the ordering of worship are jointly taken.

They *ought* to be jointly taken, because within the liturgy, priest and people are interdependent. Neither can make Eucharist without the other. The priest cannot celebrate alone, for Christian worship is the worship of the whole People of God. Nor can the people make Eucharist if there is not present a priest, a man who has been called, chosen, trained, and set aside to act before God as the chief representative of the people. That is why the term 'president' is so apposite as a description of the eucharistic celebrant. 'This word emphasizes, not what the minister *is*, but rather what he *does*. He is involved in a corporate action, in which he has a particular, distinctive role, and which he cannot do just on his own.'[11] The Dean of York goes on to quote from a document arising out of a French ecumenical discussion. The section of it entitled 'The Presidency of the Eucharist' ends with these words:

> In their mutual relations, the eucharistic gathering and its president live their dependence on the one Lord and great High Priest. In its relation to the minister, the congregation is exercising its royal priesthood conferred on it by Christ, the priest. In his relation to the congregation, the minister is living his presidency as the servant of Christ, the pastor.[12]

The congregation has a priesthood; the president exercises the role of a servant. Both the president and the people are paradoxes: but so is the whole of their worship. Both priest and people are mutually interdependent. So they must be: they are both incorporate within the one Christ whose worship they offer as they join together as an indivisible community to make Eucharist.

— ▶▼◄ —

Despite all we have said so far, there are still congregations where the liturgy of the people has become almost completely atrophied. How may they recover it? What parts of the service may properly be given to them, and how?

In the remainder of this chapter, I intend to go through the Eucharist section by section with these questions in mind. Naturally, I know the rites of the Church of England best, and I shall be using them at various points for illustration. But I make bold to hope, not only that what I here write may be of use to non-English Anglicans, but also that it may have something to say to those quite outside the Anglican fold. The skeleton of the rite (particularly in those revised rites where the influence of the Joint Liturgical Group has been felt) has become common to many services in many communions in many parts of the world, and those of us who share problems may find some common ground in the answers to them.

The service begins with the ministry of the Word. This involves both readings and sermon. It is becoming a commonplace nowadays to allow lay people to read the Bible in church, but the Bible can be communicated in other ways than by reading it. I recollect a parish weekend in a conference house a year or so ago where a group from the congregation dramatized the Gospel reading in the form of a role-play. That is one stage further along from the familiar sharing out of the Passion readings among several voices during Holy Week, and it is worth trying out as an exercise in congregational participation. It need not be 'live'; there is scope for imaginative work with a tape-recorder—wonders can be worked even with quite modest equipment.[13]

A similar treatment can be accorded to the sermon. I recollect an experiment made at a youth week in which I was involved five or six years ago, where the final Eucharist of the week was planned by all the participants. They had been learning in small groups throughout their time together, and, instead of the sermon, each of the four groups was given between two and three minutes to 'put across' to themselves and to the other groups what they had learned during the week. One group did it by means of a dramatized reading, one by way of a role-play, one through music, and one through choric dance. I found it an intensely moving and worshipful experience.

That, except as a very rare occurrence, is probably too much for the average parish; but the sermon ought to have something to say to us on the subject of 'worship and community'. Normally it will be preached by the minister, but there is no reason why it should be his own unaided work. The sermon is a declaration of the counsel or gospel of God to a particular congregation in a particular place at a particular period in its history, and if it is a good sermon, it will bear signs of that 'earthing'. The minister may be aware of what *he* wants to say, but it may be that the congregation has different needs from the ones he imagines. His theology may be too abstract for them. They may need milk instead of meat. The things that are bothering him may not be the things that are bothering them—as an African layman once said of his pastor. 'He's always scratching me where I don't itch'. Is there a solution? I believe so. Many parishes have lay groups which meet regularly for study and discussion. There is great value in letting such a group tease out the message of next Sunday's readings and for having the preacher sit in on the group (as silently as he knows how) so that the following Sunday he can preach the sermon *they* need to hear, making the points which trouble *them*. Not every time, obviously, for there can be the tyranny of a clique within a congregation every bit as oppressive as the tyranny of an insensitive priest over his congregation; and St Athanasius (unlike many of our present-day synodsmen) knew the dangers of a theology of consensus.

The Ministry of the Word continues with the Creed. This too is part of the liturgy of the people, particularly if (as in the I.C.E.T. version) it is allowed to begin 'We believe' rather than 'I believe'. The Creed is primarily the Church's creed and only secondarily the credo of the individuals who happen to make up the Church. It is not the statement of a collection of individuals who all stand up and say that each of them happens to believe in the same set of propositions. No; it is what *we* believe. The Creed is the Creed of the Christian community.

The intercessions which follow the Creed can easily involve the whole community of the faithful gathered together on a Sunday, and there are many stages of 'loosening-up' through which a congregation may pass in order to move from a priestly solo to a genuine experience of the intercessions as the Prayers of all the Faithful. The priest may begin by asking members of the congregation to supply him with intercessions which come from them and mirror their concerns, even though it will be he who is voicing them on behalf of the congregation. These intercessions may be invited and collected well in advance of the service, or things may happen as I saw once in a church where the priest went up and down the aisles with a note-book just before the Intercessions, asking for names and subjects to be included. These, he wove into an appropriate semi-extempore prayer at that point in the service.

Another way to do things is for the priest to write out intercessions for a lay person or group of lay people to speak. Or the congregation itself, through an appointed representative, can arrange for the collection of written intercessions for one of their number to use. Members of the congregation can be detailed in advance to pray in their own words (either prepared or extempore) at this point in the service. Or there may be a Quaker or a Brethren silence during which the congregation prays silently for whatever lies on each individual heart. If the congregation has become used to praying together, or if a group from within the congregation has learnt to be more articulate in its shared prayer, this is the point at which members of the congregation can be encouraged to break the silence by speaking out their own subjects for intercession.

What is done here will partly depend on how close (and how articulate) the Christian community of the congregation already is. Partly, however, it can be creative of Christian community, cementing a fellowship through an experience of shared prayer—whether silent or spoken. It needs careful and prayerful fostering. There may be times when there is need of great Christian tact in curbing the over-zealous or over-loquacious or over-repetitive member of the congregation. There is need to guard against the thoughtless churning out of cant phrases in a way which becomes boring or mechanical. It is well if a few simple rules are made and adhered to—for example, that no member of the congregation may pray more than once in each session, that prayers should consist of no more than one sentence each, and so on. These may sound arbitrary and dampening, but their existence may well be the salvation of a congregation. If the prayers of the faithful in the eucharistic assembly can be shared in an open and natural way, the travail to bring the community to this point will have been outstandingly worth while.

In the Church of England's Series 3 service, the transition from the Ministry of the Word and the Prayers to the Ministry of the Sacrament comes at the Peace. The sentence which precedes the giving of the Peace is a perfect text on the subject of Worship and Community:

> We are the Body of Christ. In the one Spirit we were all baptized into one body. Let us then pursue all that makes for peace and builds up our common life.

In some churches this is made the signal for what has become known as the 'walk-about'. The liturgy stops for five minutes whilst the Sunday School comes in. The congregation moves round the church building, talking to neighbours, welcoming newcomers, making arrangements for the week ahead, taking photographs at the font of the babies who have just been baptized, or having a brew-up of coffee at the back of the church. At first the idea may be welcomed with considerable suspicion, but gradually it can begin to loosen up the congregation and to help to make them more aware of themselves as the fellowship of the Body of Christ and of their worship as a congregationally participant affair. The Peace, the walk-about, should be seen, not as an interruption of the liturgy but as itself a liturgical expression of the fellowship of the community.

The Ministry of the Sacrament follows. Before the priest may take the elements, they have to be got to the table. The Parish Communion movement has popularized the notion that they should be brought up by lay people from the body of the church, symbolizing their own offering of their selves, their lives and labour, their work and their leisure. Michael Ramsey many years ago pointed out the danger that the action would be interpreted in terms of what he called 'a shallow and romantic sort of Pelagianism',[14] and his warning turned many priests away from the idea of experimenting with this ceremony. The danger *is* present, but it should be neutralized by the use of the sentence 'All things come from you, and of your own do we give you' (1 Chron. 29.14 as in Series 3, section 24). We can offer nothing but what God has already given us, yet the offering is none the less real and none the less *our* offering for all that. The paradox hits us again. In worship, as in the life of grace, it cannot long be avoided.

The eucharistic prayer—the prayer of consecration or of thanksgiving—is the nub of the whole rite, and it must be seen as the prayer of the whole eucharistic community, not of the priest alone. There are wrong and right ways of ensuring this. The wrong way is to have the congregation say the prayer with the priest. This blurs the real distinction between the liturgy of the president and the liturgy of the people. The priest has been set aside by ordination in order to be able to preside at the Eucharist. That is his liturgy. The people's part at this precise juncture in the service is to assent to what he does on their behalf, as their ordained representative before God, by giving his prayer their 'Amen' and making it their own. St Paul refers explicitly to the saying of 'Amen' at the *eucharistia* (1 Cor. 14.16). Though it is but a single word, its use at this point is of outstanding importance. The Church of England's Series 3 rite has a very clever way of preventing the people from mumbling it or letting it pass unsaid. The end of the Prayer of Thanksgiving is marked by a congregational response of which 'Amen' is the last word. Inattentive congregations are readily caught napping by a single word 'Amen' at the end of a long prayer by someone else; but when they have to say together the whole of the response 'Blessing and honour and glory and power be yours for ever and ever', they have been won into participation by this phrase, and their 'Amen' has at last become a congregational reality rather than a liturgiologist's desideratum.

It has always seemed a pity to me that the symbolism of the One Bread is so seldom observed in the Anglican Church. The celebrant solemnly breaks a priest's wafer, and the people (if they are using Series 3) reply, 'Though we are many, we are one body, because we all share in one bread'; and promptly they all come up to receive individual wafers which have been baked as separate pieces. What is more, in many congregations the priest and people consume wafers of different sizes, as if to accentuate the fact that what is good enough for the congregation is not good enough for the priest. Nothing, of course, could be further from the intentions of those who use priest's wafers, but the unintended symbolism speaks louder than the intended. It is reinforced when laypeople see the priest's wafer being broken so that portions of it may be used for communicating priests who are members of the congregation. If it is felt that the use of a large wafer is more convenient in that it is easier to break at the Fraction, easier to see at the Elevation, and easier to use for intinction, then let it be used also for the communion of the people. Far better, in any case, to use the large square wafers which can be readily broken into twelve or twenty-four so that it is literally true that the whole congregation shares in one bread. This is (of course) only possible with very small congregations. Best of all, do away with unleavened wafers altogether and revert to the 1662 rubric which tells us that 'the Bread [shall] be such as is usual to be eaten; but the best and purest Wheat Bread that conveniently may be gotten'. That way, we do all share in one bread, and symbolize most effectively the truth that we are all one body and worshipping as community.

Finally, the Eucharist is a meal, and meals taken by oneself are

dull affairs. Can we not sometimes restore the original setting of the
Eucharist as a community meal by putting it within the setting of a
real, rather than a purely symbolic, act of eating and drinking? As we
can see from 1 Corinthians 11, the agapé and the Eucharist were
originally very closely connected, and it was only the abuses against
which Paul inveighed which eventually resulted in their separation.
Now, only the Eucharist has survived, and if we have a parish
breakfast or a harvest supper or a stewardship dinner or any other
kind of parochial beano, we strip it of its eucharistic elements and
make it a meal rather than an agapé.

There are two schools of thought here. John Gunstone, in *The
Charismatic Prayer Group*, suggests that 'when it is not possible to
celebrate the eucharist other forms of meals may be used to invoke
God's grace on his people as they meet together' and stresses that
such meals, though they may include the passing round of a cup of
wine after the repast, are not 'intended to be a form of the
eucharist'.[15] On the other hand, Trevor Lloyd, in his booklet *Agapes
and Informal Eucharists*, shows us how an agapé can be the
combination of the Eucharist with a real meal, as was the case in the
first-century Church at Corinth. He gives some sample orders
of service.[16] His order of events is, I feel, a trifle 'bitty' in that
there are elements of the Communion service between every
course of the meal. I would prefer to have the Ministry of
the Word and intercessions before the meal, then the supper as a
whole, then the Ministry of the Sacrament followed by informal
conversation and fellowship. That, however, is a detail. The principle
that Christian fellowship-meals and the Eucharist could with
profit be combined seems to me to be self-evident and I would like to
see the custom 'take on'. John Gunstone's non-eucharistic kind
of agape seems a distinctly second-best, though it could obviously
come into its own in the absence of a priest, or for an ecumenical
group where questions of church order and discipline forbade
intercommunion.

All these are ways in which worship and community are seen to
be inextricable if the worship is Christian worship, and particularly if
it is the fully Christian worship of the Eucharist with the Ministry of

the Word, the Intercessions, and the Ministry of the Sacrament. Our
worship ought to help us

some to be apostles, some prophets, some evangelists, some
pastors and teachers, to equip God's people for work in his
service, to the building up of the body of Christ. So shall we all at
last attain to the unity inherent in our faith and our knowledge of
the Son of God—to mature manhood, measured by nothing less
than the full stature of Christ. . . . Let us speak the truth in love; so
shall we fully grow up into Christ. He is the head, and on him the
whole body depends. Bonded and knit together by every
constituent joint, the whole frame grows through the due activity
of each part, and builds itself up in love. (Eph. 4.11–13, 15–16)

4

WORSHIP AND
MISSION

Half of the paradox of worship is that we may not consider it primarily as a human activity directed towards God. God comes first. The opening words of the Te Deum have for centuries been translated into English as 'We praise thee, O God'. Dewi Morgan once reminded us that, as a translation of the phrase *Te deum laudamus*, our English version

> may be literally accurate. But as an expression of the inner meaning it falls sadly short. For the Latin puts God first. The English usurps that divine and inalienable right and puts *us* first. In doing so it illustrates, albeit unintentionally, what man has done. We act as if God has been toppled from his throne and rendered superfluous, as though God could wait until we got round to thinking of him.[1]

Behind the overstatement, there is a truth here, which has been recovered in the I.C.E.T. translation, however barbarous it may be as a piece of liturgical prose: 'You are God we praise you'.

The prevenience of God is one half of the paradox of worship. It is disastrous to forget it. But it is equally disastrous to forget the other side of the picture, and to imagine that worship is so much God's doing that it does not need to call forth human effort. In this chapter we shall try to explore the implications of that paradox as we discuss the relations between worship and mission.

When, on page 8–10 above, we looked at that vignette of the life of the early Church which we found in Acts 2.42–7, it became clear that it was improper to think of worship as the cause, and community and mission as its effects. We saw then the inadequacy of treating the human activity of shared worship as productive of fellowship and community so that more and more people want to take part in such friendly occasions. That would be to link worship with community-and-mission in a purely human way. About God we could then say, with Laplace, that we had no need of that hypothesis. Not only would he not come first: he would not necessarily come into the picture at all.

Is there a way out? One way would be via that quotation from Mollie Batten (see page 25 above) which spoke of the local Church and its worship as being there as

> a place for the laity to call in for their briefing, for their work in the world; for the sacraments through which they will be cleaned and refitted for duty; for the prayers in which they will . . . receive new light for their witness.

Worship *empowers* us for mission. It gives us our marching orders for the real work of mission, which takes place not in the service itself but outside and afterwards. 'What I say to you in the dark you must repeat in broad daylight; what you hear whispered you must shout from the house-tops' (Matt. 10.27). In worship we hear things said by God in the secret place which it is our duty to proclaim in the market-place. God, whom we meet in our act of worship, gives us the motive power to do the proclamation. Without the worship, the mission would be powerless; without the mission, the worship would be a sham. Without God, neither could take place.

This is getting us nearer to an adequate formulation, but it is still far from being the whole truth. God has been brought in—but only (as it were) dragged in because it would be unseemly not to find a place for him. He is still curiously external to the whole affair. He is simply the mechanism by which the cause is related to the effect. Worship only leads to mission because it is God who has been invoked as the link. Without him, worship would be powerless to lead to mission, just as a car (however excellent its engine) would be powerless to travel without petrol.

What has gone wrong is that worship has been degraded to the status of a means, rather than an end in itself. And when worship becomes a means—even a means to doing something which God wants doing—its whole flavour is subtly altered, and for the worse. The paradox has its centre of gravity shifted towards the activist end of the spectrum, and 'mission' tends to become narrowed down either to evangelism or to Christian social work in the world. These are a vital *part* of mission, but if they are treated as the *whole* of mission, the richness of the concept is in danger of disappearing.

If we are to get ourselves out of trouble, we need to find a starting-point of a less humanistic and activist kind. I believe our difficulties have largely stemmed from trying to find *relationships* between worship, community, and mission, whereas the three concepts are so closely tied together that even the relationship of cause and effect is too loose for the purpose. Instead, we should be attempting to find a *unity* of which worship, community, and mission are different aspects; and I believe that this unity is nothing less than God himself. In him, worship, community, and mission coinhere.

We hinted as much in Chapter 1 (pages 9–10) where we asserted the divine priority in all these activities. Worship is something God does. Christ baptizes us in the Spirit, adding new members to his body. Christ is the unseen President at every Eucharist, present in his body and his blood, giving himself to those who feed upon him. Worship is a prevenient activity of God and (the paradox of worship being like the paradox of grace) it is only a human activity insofar as God is working within us to urge us to worship. The same is true of community. Christian fellowship is the expression of being Christ's body. It is not something we create but something of God into which we enter. Mission, likewise, is the nature of the God whose activity we join when we worship and whose body we are if he has called us.

If all this is true, then we have to look to the doctrine of God for an understanding of mission. Mission is what God *is*, before it is what the Church *does*. In the words of Douglas Webster,

> Mission is central to theology because it springs out of the character of God. . . . It is rooted in the doctrine of the Trinity, not in the doctrine of the Church.[2]

Worship is a missionary activity because God is a missionary God. But before we go forward to explore that statement in terms of the nature of God, we need to guard against construing it as meaning that the purpose of worship is to attract newcomers into the

Christian community. That would be inadequate both in terms of worship and in terms of mission. In terms of worship it would be inadequate because it would—once more—degrade worship into a means towards an end. It is not, not even when that end is so desirable an end as evangelization. Even when we recognize the paradox whereby it is God who does the evangelizing through the services we arrange, we do a disservice to the activity of worship by making it secondary to any other activity. The purpose of worship is to be sought within itself and not outside itself. We cannot say that worship leads to mission. We must find some way of saying that worship *is* mission. It is here that we discover the other aspect of the inadequacy of our early statement. It is inadequate on the 'mission' side as well, because it narrows 'mission' down to 'evangelism'. Evangelism is only one of the many strands which together make up the mission of God. The point can be made by another quotation from Douglas Webster:

> Mission derives from a Latin root and ranges round the whole concept of sending and being sent. Its Greek equivalent is found in our words apostle and apostolic. Evangelism derives from a Greek root meaning Good News. . . . Mission has about it a sense of action, posture, or process: its root is a verb, with the idea of motion or movement. But evangelism is based on a noun: it is centred in news which must be reported in words, about a person, an event, a series of events.[3]

There are thus many things about the mission of Jesus which were other than evangelism—there was healing, there was cleansing, there was liberation, and there was proclaiming. 'All evangelism is mission. Not all mission is evangelism.' What was true of the mission of Christ when he came to this earth remains true of our own mission. Christ

> sends his church to do many things. Their totality is the Christian mission. Of these things, evangelism has its unique importance. Healing, teaching, baptising, liberating, protesting, working for peace and justice, feeding the hungry, reconciling those at variance, are all essential parts of mission.[4]

The subject 'Worship and Mission' is therefore wider and richer than 'Worship and Evangelism'. That does not, however, mean that we can take shelter in a wide generalization and forget the evangelistic effects of our worship. The general includes the particular; it does not make it insignificant. Worship which is unconcerned about the winning of the world for God is not true Christian worship. A worshipping body which is self-satisfied with its own inwardly-directed fellowship is a Satanic counterfeit of Christian worship, all the more dangerous because Satan, masquerading as an angel of light (2 Cor. 11.14) tries to fool people into believing that this close-knit community is a Christian fellowship when it is in fact not showing that most essential mark of Christ, a concern that those outside its ranks may be brought in. There are, alas!, too many congregations like that. Outwardly they may appear to thrive, but they have the seeds of death within them. Evangelism may only be one part of mission, but it is a part which is a touch-stone of the rest. Although 'Worship and Mission' is not about how to devise evangelistic services, it must include a consideration of the evangelistic impact of what we do when we worship. It is an impact, however, which is best made within a wider understanding of the nature of God as a nature which is mission. If we want to understand the missionary character of Christian worship, we need to start by looking at the missionary character of the Christian's God.

The most immediately obvious characteristic of the God of the Bible is that he is a *sending* God. In the writings of the Old Testament we are shown how he sends an astonishing variety of things, from the plagues of Egypt to the swarms of 'hopper and grub and locust, my great army which I sent against you' (Joel 2.25); but more significant than the sending of natural phenomena or sub-human armies is the sending of men and angels as God's human and super-human prophets and messengers. It would be tedious to detail examples. Five minutes with the concordance will supply more than enough data to substantiate this claim. What is more, God's nature as a sending God was not for the Old Testament writers simply a matter of past history but one of future promise. They believed that his sending would come to a climax when he would send a messenger to clear the way before him and when, suddenly, the Lord whom men sought would come to his temple (Mal. 3.1).

When we pass from the Old to the New Testament, we find that what happened was even more astonishing than the most far-seeing of the prophets had expected, and it teaches us something even more profound about the sending nature of God. God does not only send outside himself, as it were; he is the Holy Trinity, and within the very being of the Trinity himself there is this characteristic of sending and being sent. The inner nature of the Trinity is a sending nature.[5] God was not content to send envoys and messengers, he

> sent his own Son, born of a woman, born under the law, to purchase freedom for the subjects of the law, in order that we might attain the status of sons. To prove that you are sons, God has sent into our hearts the Spirit of his Son, crying 'Abba! Father!' (Gal. 4.4–6)

God sends his Son, he sends the Spirit, in order that we may be adopted as his sons. The Trinity coinheres by the act of sending. Mission is no external accident; it is part of the substantive nature of God.

The *purpose* of the divine mission is elsewhere expressed in terms of reconciliation. This is what has been accomplished by the sending of the Son, and this is what Christians are sent into the world to continue. Not that we are allowed to lose sight of the paradox: it is not we who are agents of reconciliation, except insofar as it is God who works in and through us.

> From first to last this has been the work of God. He has reconciled us men to himself through Christ, and he has enlisted us in this service of reconciliation. What I mean is, that God was in Christ reconciling the world to himself, no longer holding men's misdeeds against them, and that he has entrusted us with the message of reconciliation. (2 Cor. 5.18 f)

The purpose of God's mission is reconciliation. The *means* of reconciliation was the atoning death of Christ. Paul makes this particularly clear in the verses immediately preceding and immediately following the passage we have just quoted:

His purpose in dying for all was that men, while still in life, should cease to live for themselves, and should live for him who for their sake died and was raised to life. . . . Be reconciled to God! Christ was innocent of sin, and yet for our sake God made him one with the sinfulness of men, so that in him we might be made one with the goodness of God himself. (2 Cor. 5.15, 20 f)

The next question is how this past event which is the means of reconciliation can be made present to men and effective in the current moment. The answer is that it is in the Eucharist that we proclaim the Lord's death until he comes (1 Corinthians 11.26). The atoning death of Christ thereby becomes a contemporary event. In the Eucharist we make *anamnesis* of that crucial moment. We re-call it so that it is once more (as always) effective for our reconciliation to God. In the eucharistic action we are both expressing and effecting the mission of God, the reason why he sent his Son into the world, the act of reconciliation between God and man.

Yet (and here comes the paradox again) it is not *we* who make the re-call effective, but God, who has given us this rite as the means whereby we can apply to the whole of mankind the benefits of that one perfect and sufficient sacrifice, oblation, and satisfaction for the whole world's sins. That is what God's mission is about. He sent his Son into the world for the reconciliation of the whole world to himself; that is what he sent the Spirit of his Son into our hearts for; that is what the Spirit sends us out into the world for. That is the whole *raison d'être* of the missionary Church. The Eucharist is a missionary activity in that it expresses *and effects* God's mission to us and our mission to the sinful and sinning world. We cannot therefore separate the worship of the Church from the mission of the Church without being untrue to both.

It is therefore possible (and indeed not only possible but proper) to speak of mission and cult, apostolicity and priesthood, in one and the same breath. This is what Paul does when, writing to the Romans, he tells them that God's

grace has made me a minister of Christ Jesus to the Gentiles; my *priestly service* is the *preaching of the gospel* of God, and it falls to me to offer the Gentiles to him as an acceptable sacrifice, consecrated by the Holy Spirit (Rom. 15.16).

Here the link is between priesthood and that part of mission which is contained within evangelism, but the connection between worship and mission is nonetheless there. A better example comes in the Epistle to the Hebrews where it is said (3.1) of a greater than Paul that he is 'the Apostle and High Priest of the religion we profess'. The whole of this Epistle, indeed, can be read as an expression of the link between worship and mission, between high priesthood and apostolicity. As with Paul in 2 Corinthians 5, the common term is that of reconciliation. Reconciliation between man and God is the reason for the mission of God, and it is also the function of the High Priest.[6]

The author of the Epistle to the Hebrews points out to us that the priest in the Old Testament was the man who stood as intermediary between God and the people. The High Priest went up to the Holy of Holies once a year— not without blood—on the Day of Atonement, the day of reconciliation. There he found himself at the mystical place where (as it were) the gap between man and God was annulled and the primordial harmony re-established.

That ancient dispensation of the former Covenant was inadequate, and the author of the Epistle ruthlessly fastens on its limitations. It was a system of ritual offerings to atone for ritual offences. The more serious barriers created by even the venial sins of fallen humanity, let alone wilful rebellion against the known will of God, stood outside the system (Heb. 9.8–10). Even within this limited sphere, the efficacy of what the High Priest could do was far from perfect. He was sinful, so that he had to offer for his own sins as well as for those of the people (Heb. 7.27); his offering prevailed only for a time, so that it had to be repeated year by year (Heb. 9.25); and he was mortal so that he had to be replaced by a new High Priest on his death (Heb. 7.23).

Why not then do away altogether with this system of limited value? That is not possible, for it has within it a germ of a great truth. That link between the reconciling mission of God and the worship of Jewry may be imperfect, but it is indispensable because it is a copy

and shadow or symbol (Heb. 8.5, 9.24, 10.1). Like the shadows in
Plato's cave, the sacrificial order tells us something about how things
are in the archetypical realm of which the earthly tabernacle is a
reflection. What we need to do is to see through it to its heavenly
original. This we can do when we fix our eyes on Jesus (Heb. 12.2), a
high priest for ever in the succession of Melchizedek (Heb 6.20). 'He
has taken his seat at the right hand of the throne of Majesty in the
heavens, a ministrant in the real sanctuary, the tent pitched by the
Lord and not by man' (Heb. 8.1–2). As the earthly High Priest went
through the veil to the Holy of Holies, into God's presence on our
behalf, so Jesus

> by his death on the day of his perfect atonement for all sin, the Son
> of Man, our great high priest, though no priest of the order of
> Levi, ruptures the barrier between the sacred and the profane, the
> divine and the human, the transcendent and the incarnate, and
> leaves a breach through which ordinary men may storm into the
> sanctuary.[7]

Because he is both very man and very God, Jesus is able to
bridge the gap between the humanity of the High Priest and the
divinity of God. By being what he is, he effects atonement in the
sacrifice of his own blood and reconciles the otherwise
irreconcilable. Thus it is that the Epistle to the Hebrews unites the
language of the cult and the language of mission by talking about the
effecting of reconciliation through priesthood. Although there is
surprisingly little explicitly eucharistic reference in the epistle,[8] we
cannot help but refer its insights to the sacrament whereby that
atonement is made the object of our *anamnesis* and made present
and effective to us. Mission and cult are as inseparable as the unity of
our undivided God.

— ▶▼◀ —   •

We have so far spoken of the mission of God as a mission of
reconciliation, but have only dealt with one part of that
reconciliation—the reconciliation between God and man. The
mission of God is wider than this, for it necessarily involves also the
reconciliation between man and man and between man and the

natural world. In terms of our earlier metaphor, we must be concerned with a horizontal reconciliation as well as with a vertical one. That truth can be expressed equally well in terms of worship as in terms of mission, and we find both in the pages of the New Testament. In terms of mission,

> If a man says, 'I love God', while hating his brother, he is a liar.... He who loves God [i.e. he who is reconciled in the vertical dimension] must also love his brother [i.e. be reconciled in the horizontal dimension also]. (1 John 4.20 f)

That verse, translated from the language of mission into that of worship, becomes

> If, when you are bringing your gift to the altar, you suddenly remember that your brother has a grievance against you, leave your gift where it is before the altar. First go and make your peace with your brother, and only then come back and offer your gift. (Matt. 5.23 f)

When we miss out on the horizontal dimension—reconciliation between man and man—mission is narrowed down to proselytism and worship is contracted into an introverted pietism. In either case, the 'bite' of Christianity is lost, and the world knows that it can safely ignore a Church which is not doing anything to threaten its autonomy. The dangers need to be spelt out and the warning signals recognized.

Proselytism was the downfall of the old Israel. It was a noble and genuine attempt to universalize the acknowledged sovereignty of Jehovah, but it was not mission. Like a counterfeit coin, it was close enough to mission for many people to mistake it for the genuine article; but for Christians this approach is no longer legal tender and it does not deliver the goods. Proselytism is exemplified in Zechariah 8.20–3:

> Nations and dwellers in great cities shall yet come; people of one city shall come to those of another and say, 'Let us go and entreat the favour of the LORD, and resort to the LORD of Hosts; and I will come too.' So great nations and mighty peoples shall resort to the LORD of Hosts in Jerusalem and entreat his favour. These

are the words of the LORD of Hosts: In those days, when ten men
from nations of every language pluck up courage, they shall pluck
the robe of a Jew and say, 'We will go with you because we have
heard that God is with you'.

That sounds like mission, but it is not. It sounds like reconciliation,
but it is in fact spiritual aggrandizement. It treats the other man, not
as a brother, but as a tool. Instead of seeking a genuine reconciliation
between God and man, it uses religion as a cloak for saying, 'You
can only be reconciled with God on my terms'. Nations who want to
entreat the favour of the LORD can only do so if they leave their own
land and go to Jerusalem. There they must 'pluck the robe of a Jew'
(a phrase which 'probably means to "accept the Jewish way of life"
and so, perhaps, to "become a proselyte"')[9] and establish a
synagogue—where the conduct of public worship required ten adult
males.[10] There is here no attempt to find common ground with the
religious aspirations of other nations. A man must be drawn out of
his own world and come into Judaism. Proselytism does not really
respect the other man, and it therefore cannot be a genuine tool for
reconciliation between man and man. The more dangerous
road—and the one which takes very much longer to travel—is the
way of dialogue; but that way is the only one along which there is
any permanent hope of success.

The saying of Jesus reported in Matthew 8.11 sails dangerously
near to proselytism. 'Many, I tell you', the verse goes, 'will come
from east and west to feast with Abraham, Isaac, and Jacob in the
kingdom of Heaven'. The Synoptic Gospels present Jesus to us
clearly as 'a thorough Jew, who thought as a Jew and who worked
only among fellow-members of the twelve tribes'.[11] David Edwards
suggests that Jesus himself used the imagery of the Old Testament
(and obviously he is thinking of Zechariah 8) in which to clothe his
references to future appeals to the Gentiles, as he did not himself
have in mind a mission to Gentiles in Gentile territory. We need to be
clear, however, that this restriction 'resulted from the limitations of
time and energy [within the confines of the historic ministry of Jesus
of Nazareth]; it was not a matter of profound and permanent
principle'.[12] He did not, by the use of the imagery from Zechariah,

rule out the possibility of a wider mission. Indeed, the very existence of his Church bears witness to the fact that had the possibility not been actualized, the whole mission of Christ would have been stultified.

Judaism had a mission and a vocation.[13] It accepted its vocation but eventually it failed in its mission. The *vocation* of Judaism was to exist, in order to show that God had called to him a nation. Israel accepted that vocation. Its *mission* was to show, through acceptance of that vocation and an extension of its terms, that God could call to himself *every* nation out of the whole inhabited earth.

> The people of Israel were singled out, ... not to present themselves to the rest of the world as the nation through which God's redeeming love would be mediated, *but* to be a symbol of how God would also deal redemptively with other nations.[14]

In that mission Israel failed. Instead, it tried to draw other nations into itself. It compassed sea and land to make one proselyte (Matt. 23.15) and it refused to universalize the calling of God.

We should not think ourselves superior to Israel. We are guilty of the same error every time we act as though our message is 'come to us and be saved'. It is the attitude of the parson who does not go out visiting 'because', as he says, 'they know where the Vicarage is if they want me'. It is the attitude of the believer who has learnt a pre-arranged programme giving all the properly approved steps of the way to conversion and who insists that anybody who does not conform to that programme is of doubtful standing before the Lord. He has forgotten that there is a divine part to the paradox of mission and that God is supremely unpredictable. God's truth and his methods are so multi-faceted that he can lead every man to himself in that man's own unique way. Pre-determined methods of proselytism are of very limited success and of even more limited value.

There are other monuments to a proselytizing attitude. Some of them, like those magnificent pseudo-Gothic cathedrals in far-off mission stations, will be with us for a very long time to remind us of the disastrous but short-term success which attended our confusion of mission with Westernization. In their way they are as ludicrously out-of-place as the trousers which the missionaries of the same era wrapped round their African converts' legs. But the proselytizing attitude dies hard. It is still with us when we condemn the World Council of Churches for looking at the world and its politics from a Third World viewpoint. It is all part of the attitude of the man who cannot be bothered to be reconciled with his fellow-man and who thinks that reconciliation will have happened when he has graciously allowed all the movement to be made by the other, and all the concessions to be made to him. We like the kind of Christianity and the kind of worship we have inherited, and we are so often blind to its insularity. It is hard (but necessary) to realize how profoundly it has been moulded by the culture that surrounds it and how it needs to be transformed if it is to become a true part of any other culture.

And so we proselytize. Instead of allowing God the freedom to carry out *his* mission, we interfere by seeking adherents to our *own* cause and our *own* opinions. Proselytizing is cosy. Mission is uncertain, uncharted, dangerous. Proselytism is centripetal—'Gentiles shall *come* to thy light, and kings to the brightness of thy rising' (Isa. 60.3 A.V.). Mission is centrifugal—'*Go* forth therefore and make all nations my disciples' (Matt. 28.19); 'you will receive power when the Holy Spirit comes upon you; and you will bear witness for me in Jerusalem, and all over Judaea and Samaria, and away to the ends of the earth' (Acts 1.8).

When mission is reduced to proselytism, then worship becomes perverted into introspective pietism. If we are satisfied that our community contains everything necessary for the salvation of everybody who may conceivably come to join it; if we keep open house, but only for those who think and act as we do; then we are never going to be challenged by any new and uncomfortable ideas, and our worship will be pietistic, and designed to insulate us from the disturbance caused by intrusion. Pietism concentrates on the emotions and inward aspirations of the worshippers. Its worship is 'what a man does with his solitariness'. The structures of the world will allow that kind of worship to continue, and perhaps even accord it an amused tolerance. But let worship once show itself as the expression of a community which believes that 'the sovereignty of the world has passed to our Lord and his Christ and he shall reign for ever and ever!' (Rev. 11.15), and there is trouble in the world, because the world recognizes the threat to its sovereignty.

Pietism concentrates on God's reconciliation with the worshipper, and misses out on God's desire to be reconciled with the whole world—a reconciliation which can come about only if man and man are reconciled in the real, concrete, and actual structures of the world. In bread and wine we should see the hallowing of worldly matter, the hallowing of man's work and of his joy, the hallowing—within the community of the Body of Christ—of human community; the calling to mend broken relationships, to straighten twisted threads, to reconcile warring factions, to ensure that justice runs like rivers and righteousness as a mountain stream, to bind the brokenhearted and release the captive. In the bread and wine of the Eucharist we see the declaration that there is no aspect of man's humanity and his society which cannot be atoned and reconciled to God in Christ, no aspect of his relationships with his fellow-man where he may not be atoned with and reconciled to the rest of humanity. Worship involves the continuous effort towards the reconciliation of man with man. And—since the world is in the grip of the Evil One—that spells trouble when the world realizes what true worship entails.

Some years ago, I came across an item in the *Church Times* which I found so nauseatingly compelling that I cut it out and kept it for reference. It was reporting a statement in *Izvestia* to the effect that

> most Russian clergymen are endeavouring to be loyal to all the measures taken by the Soviet Government in the sphere of domestic and foreign policy.

It went on to define the freedom of conscience which the Russian churches enjoyed.

> In our country freedom of conscience does not mean . . . that the activity of religious associations must be unrestricted and that they can do anything they like—without regard for the legal ordinances of our country. The law insists that religion must restrict its activity to satisfying the religious needs of believers.[15]

More recently, we have seen the same kind of attitude on the part of the governments of Eastern Europe documented on page after page of Trevor Beeson's intensely moving chronicle entitled *Discretion and Valour*.[16] The state authorities in those countries

> prefer a Christian witness which is totally confined to liturgy and religion in the narrowest sense of the word. So the ... Communists agree on one vital point: 'Religion has nothing to do with politics, nor with public life. It is a private individual affair.' Persecution arises where the church sees its mission in the broader biblical sense, and understandably so because it comes into conflict with historical materialism.[17]

Introverted religiosity—worship without mission—is no threat. Real religion—worship which is the obverse of the coin whose reverse is mission 'in the broader biblical sense of the word—worship which realizes that what *Izvestia* called 'the religious needs of believers' include reconciliation of man to God and man to man and the reconciliation of the world's structures of government, power, and politics to God's plan for mankind—that kind of worship and that kind of religion call forth from the Russian and East European authorities the timeworn cry of *non licet esse vos*—Christians are not allowed to exist. But that is the only kind of worship worth offering.

> True worship is an announcement to all the tyrants that against them stands a critic and a victor. It is an announcement that opposition to false gods and false gospels is valid and worthwhile. . . . True worship is not an anaesthetic, a frivolous diversion of energy from the battles for justice and righteousness. . . . Far from being an anaesthetic, worship should be the most powerful political stimulant of all.[18]

Those words of John D. Davies speak all the more eloquently to us when we realize that the book from which they are taken began life as a series of lectures given when the author was serving in South Africa—a place which, God knows, needs the message of mission which is the message of total reconciliation.

So far we have looked at mission (seen in terms of reconciliation) within two kinds of relationship—the relationship between man and God and that between man and man. There is a third relationship within which reconciliation is needed, and that too must be seen as part of the Christian mission. It is the relationship of man with nature. This aspect of reconciliation hardly needs stressing nowadays, so popular have the causes of ecology and conservation recently become. All the more cause for penitence that the gospel of reverence for nature has for so long been so badly obscured. For generations we misinterpreted the command about filling the earth and subduing it and ruling over every living thing that moves upon the earth (Gen. 1.28) as though the rulers had no responsibilities and that over which they ruled had no rights. This was a situation in which the mission of reconciliation was desperately needed. At last the balance has begun to swing the right way. It will not be completely put right until the final Day, because part of the result of the Fall is that 'the whole created universe groans in all its parts as if in the pangs of childbirth' (Rom. 8.22), awaiting its redemption. Yet we have an earnest of the eschatological moment, a firstfruits of reconciled nature; we have it in the material elements of bread and wine when they become in Christian worship the sacrament of the Body and Blood of their Maker. In Christian worship, reconciliation between man and matter is begun, through the action of that God whose mission is to reconcile all things in himself. No one who joins in Eucharistic worship should be unmindful of his duty towards God's material creation.

We have been exploring the link between our worship and God's mission (or, if you prefer it, between God's worship and our mission) in terms of the concept of reconciliation. We have already shown one way of understanding how the Eucharist expresses and effects God's work of reconciliation, so that we participate in mission by our very act of making Eucharist. There is another way in which we may understand the same truth, and that is by seeing each Eucharist as a renewal of our baptism. The case has been worked out in great detail by Gordon Davies in his book *Worship and Mission*,[19] so that here we need do no more than outline his case.

Baptism, no less than the Eucharist, proclaims the Lord's reconciling death till he comes. It is an entry into Christ's death and resurrection, as St Paul points out:

When we were baptized into union with Christ Jesus we were

baptized into his death. . . . In dying as he died, he died to sin,
once for all, and in living as he lives, he lives to God. In the same
way you must regard yourselves as dead to sin and alive to God,
in union with Christ Jesus. (Rom. 6.3, 10–11)

Baptism immerses us into the reconciling mystery of Christ's death-
and-resurrection, and thereby anoints us with the Spirit to equip us
for mission.

Until men and women are drawn into the missionary enterprise of
the Church, they do not discover the meaning of their baptism.[20]

Each Eucharist may be considered as a renewing and refreshing of
our baptism, declaring and making continually effective in the life of
the Church that truth which was enacted at our baptism. The
Eucharist renews us within the baptismal life and re-establishes us
within the baptismal pattern of life-through-death, Christ's-life-
through-Christ's-death, within the reconciling love of God known in
his mission of Cross and resurrection. Our commitment to Christ,
whose obedience to God was an obedience to mission, is renewed at
every Eucharist because we are there matured in our incorporation
within the body into which we were enfolded at our baptism.

— ►▲◄ —

Mission, therefore, forms an inevitable dimension to Christian
worship. We participate in God's mission as we join in Christian
worship. That is one side of the paradox. The other side is that it is up
to us to ensure that the dimension becomes so explicit within the
worship we offer that it can take effect, through our lives, in the lives
of others. In the last chapter we went through the structure of the
Eucharist with the idea of community in mind, and saw how the
service was permeated with this concept and how it could be the
more explicitly expressed. The same is true of mission, as we shall
now see.

In the Ministry of the Word, we listen to Scripture and Sermon.
The dimension of mission in them is immediately obvious.

The Bible is the record of a sending God; consequently to read
from it, in the course of worship, is to present the hearers with an

account of the *missio Dei* in the past, which becomes a summons to participate in it in the present. The historical facts become contemporary realities; they are taken up into the lives of those who listen. To know what God has done in history is to be assisted to the recognition of what he is doing today and so to be enabled to join him in his mission in the world.[21]

The sermon should expound the meaning of the scripture passages and 'earth' them in the present.

The gospel is about things happening to people in particular historical situations: it is not just the filtering through of timeless ideas from a remote world where there are no real people. If one cannot tell the period or context in which a theologian is writing, the chances are that he is not truly a theologian at all.[22]

The same is even more true if for 'theologian' we substitute 'preacher'. The sermon takes the Mission of God from its scriptural context and translates it into the contemporary mission of God's people. Both lections and sermon help to stir our imagination and move our will to unite ourselves with this sending God and to become conscious of (and co-operative in) our part in his mission.

The Ministry of the Word continues with the recitation of the Creed. The Creed is not primarily a set of theological and metaphysical dogmas, even though in the past it may have been used as a means of excluding from the Church's fellowship those whose belief was unorthodox. If it were seen purely in a propositional way, it *would* deserve to be described as the badge of a proselytizing sect which wanted people to share its opinions. But it is not. It is primarily a rehearsal of God's missionary *acts* in relation to us, as he sent his Son and sends his Spirit for our reconciliation. It is a summary of the *kerygma* of mission; a declaration of God's sending love, and an invitation to us to partake in his eternal mission to mankind.

The intercessions follow upon the Creed. These too are a part of God's mission, because they are a participation in the divine action for the world. We do not only pray *for* mission, we engage *in* mission by praying. In some mysterious way which continues to be a stumbling-block to the philosophers and to defy logic, and yet is simply *known* by the praying soul to be true, our intercessions release God's reconciling work in his world. Maybe it is true that God would grant our desires for the doing of his work even if we decided not to pray, but no praying man would even *want* that to be a reason for giving up his practice of intercession. In any case, it might be true that God (in a kind of kenotic self-limitation) had decided not to act until the requisite volume of prayer had been offered. Certainly the Biblical injunctions to prayer seem to assume some such situation. Prayer, and the relation of the divine initiative to the human act within prayer, forms as much of a paradox as any other aspect of the Christian life.

So we pray, and forward God's mission by so doing. And we pray for every man for whom God has a concern. That is why I welcome the intercessory prayers in the new rites of the Church of England. Within its eucharistic intercessions, the 1662 Book of Common Prayer had us praying only for Christ's Church (and, indeed, only for that portion of it militant here on earth). Because of this limitation, the text of the prayer could only include a mention of *Christian* kings, princes, and governors. The more recent rites have removed this serious constriction, and have widened the intercessions to be as broad as the mission of God. We pray now 'for the church and for the world'. That includes Christian kings, princes, and governors, but it also includes those who ignore, or deny, or even persecute the Christian Church. In so doing, we do but follow the injunction of our Lord himself.

> You have learned that they were told, 'Love your neighbour, hate your enemy.' But what I tell you is this: Love your enemies and pray for your persecutors; only so can you be children of your heavenly Father, who makes his sun rise on good and bad alike, and sends the rain on the honest and the dishonest. (Matt. 5.43–5)

This should be true of all intercession, but more particularly of the intercessions within the Eucharist. At the Eucharist, the mission of God expressed in the whole service should be mirrored *in parvo* within the intercessions. In the words of Max Thurian,

> to celebrate the eucharist with all its intercessory power is to

accomplish an essential part of the Church's mission. When the eucharist is celebrated with a fervent intercessory intention to the conversion of the people in whose midst the Christian community is at worship, it has a missionary efficacy because of the union effected in the memorial between Christ the Intercessor and those named in the eucharistic action. . . . The Church bears before God, in the eucharist, the names of those for whom she has a mission to intercede and she offers them to the blessing and salvation of God.[23]

The mission of God in the Eucharist continues with confession and absolution.

Confession and absolution are not simply a part of the preparation for mission. They are that, certainly; the worshippers are cleansed by God's forgiveness so that they can be better vehicles for God's missionary activity. But confession and absolution are more than acts *preparatory to* mission. They are examples of God in action, of God *in* mission. The absolution is a part of God's mission in that God expresses and effects his forgiveness and reconciliation through it.

What is more, the mission expressed and effected through the absolution is a wider mission than the mission to the worshippers there assembled. The whole world is bound up together in sin and guilt and blame which are impossible to apportion individually. Indeed, it is often the case that the greatest (collective) sins can be perpetrated by men who think of themselves as decent and honest and law-abiding citizens. If they were able to see the full story of the use made of their actions, they might revolt—except that, even then, they would probably find themselves completely powerless to do anything other than acquiesce and continue. This applies most spectacularly to the German who supported his country and its Government in the 1940s, or to the Russian who did not make himself into a martyr against the policies of Stalin, but if we think it does not also apply to ourselves today, we are sadly deceived. We are tied up, inextricably, in a nexus of international trade and economics. Whether we like it or not, every penny in our bank account helps to maintain governments (for example, in South Africa) whose policies we may deplore as unChristian. We may react by refusing personally to trade with countries of which we disapprove. If we do so, we are probably thereby hitting and hurting, not the oppressors, but those whom we most need and desire to help. It is the people who are already downtrodden and oppressed who will be the first (and the worst) to be hit by trade recessions. We cannot opt out of responsibility without opting out of civilized society altogether— only an uninhabited desert island is remote enough. In this inter-dependent world, no one's hands can be clean.

All this is part of the agony in the heart of God, as he loves his world and longs for justice and mercy, and sees no human individual unaffected by the actions of all others. That is why the confession of sin in public worship can never be simply a private and individual confession. We must, and we can, properly confess, not only our own sins (as far as we are aware of them) but also the unconfessed sins of the whole unbelieving world, for the world's forgiveness. The mission of God is a mission for the world, and it is not for us to narrow that down.

> God loved the world so much that he gave his only Son, that everyone who has faith in him may not die but have eternal life. It was not to judge the world that God sent his Son into the world, but that through him the world might be saved. (John 3.16 f)

That total mission of God for the whole world lies at the back of the

> general confession, in which the congregation becomes the representative of the whole of fallen humanity, and in which the 'we' includes not only those who confess but those who refuse to confess and those who feel no need to confess. All mankind is bound together in the same bundle of humanity, and all need the same cleansing power of God.[24]

The Ministry of the Word is linked with the Ministry of the Sacrament by the Peace. The celebrant wishes the Peace of God on to the congregation, and they return it to him. So far we have been using the word 'reconciliation' to express the purpose of God's mission to the world. An equally Biblical word, and one which is rich in meaning, is the word 'peace'. This, too, expresses the purpose of

God's mission. When he sent his Son to earth, the song of the angels was 'Glory to God in highest heaven, and on earth his peace for men on whom his favour rests' (Luke 2.14). Peace means man at one with God, man at one with man, man at one with nature. It is more than a state of absence of conflict. It is positive, not negative. It is the highest possible state of well-being, in which the primordial harmony has been restored to the earth and in which God's purposes have been perfectly achieved. To wish 'peace' upon a person is to commit oneself to the mission of God and to vow to do everything in one's power to help bring it about.

Of the Ministry of the Sacrament itself, little now needs to be said, for we have set forward our case in the earlier part of this chapter. Here are the eucharistic actions, the taking, blessing, breaking, and sharing of the bread and wine. The eucharistic prayer, the Great Thanksgiving, sets forth the mission of God in creation and redemption, and re-enacts its crucial core. Here, more than anywhere else on earth, we become identified with the whole reason why our sending God became involved with this earth of his.

Finally, the closing words of the Mass, which give it its title. *Ite, missa est!* Perhaps we thought that the title 'Mass' was a fortuitous and meaningless word; but in fact it emphasizes the whole of the relationship between Eucharist and mission which it has been the aim of this chapter to explore. It means 'the dismissal'; the sending back into the world for mission of the gathered worshippers. It is the call to them to go out and do something about the mission which has been articulated and expressed through their act of worship. The association between the words 'Mass' and 'mission' is one which is valid at a far deeper level than the etymological. Mass and mission, worship and reconciliation, cult and atonement, are inseparable. If we are Christians, we must see to it that God's mission is mirrored in God's worship. Baptism and the Eucharist express and effect that mission. It is up to us to ensure that the way we express our rite and clothe it in words and actions brings this truth home to the worshippers. There is then a good chance that that mission will spread from our lips into our lives, and a rite of reconciliation will be performed by a reconciling and reconciled community.

5

WORSHIP AND
MYSTERY

There has been one enormous gap in our discussion of worship so far. Apart from the occasional hint here and there that things might be otherwise, we have been describing worship as though it were a coolly rational activity in which men engage in a detached and almost academic manner. We have talked about ways in which our worship should be planned so that it echoes our beliefs, or expresses our community, or furthers the mission in which we are engaged. True, we have also talked of the paradox whereby God's prevenience in all these activities needs to be recognized, but have we given due weight to what worship, considered as a confrontation between man and God, is *like*? What does it feel like for a man to be face to face with God?

The moment we ask this sort of question, the whole flavour of our discussion changes abruptly. A man's relation to God is of an entirely different quality from his relation with his father, or his employer, or even with his bank manager. It has within it the element of respect, but it goes beyond that. There is—and this is primary, not accidental—the element of awe. When man meets his maker, his worship touches the brink of mystery. When *that* is realized, we suddenly feel as if all our learned discussions are no more than profane babblings. We have been prattling about things which lie beyond our thinking, beyond our imagination. We are out of our depth, and below us lie ten thousand fathoms of ocean. The living mystery of God is something we shall never be able to plumb. When the profundity of it dawns upon us, all our easy talk is hushed.

If that were all there was to it, the only possible response would be silence and this chapter could end here. Worship would be a matter of being caught up into the awareness of the Wholly Other, the ineffable being between whom and man there is an infinite qualitative difference. Perhaps this is true of some kinds of worship. It cannot be the case with the worship of the Christian. He knows God in a paradoxical way; for him, God is known as the deity who has become incarnate. The Christian God is not *wholly* Other, and the gap between the Christian and his God is not infinite and qualitative, because in Jesus, the humanity of the worshipper has been taken up into the very divinity of his God. Man has been made in the image of God, and the divinity contains within himself the humanity of the Incarnate.

This fact can give us the courage to explore even the paradox of mystery. Human comprehension can never encompass the mystery of God, so we shall probably not get very far; but we are bound to make an attempt, or we shall be ignoring the most vital dimension of our worship. How can we see to it that our worship acknowledges the mystery of exploration into God, feeds upon it, and fosters it? How do we bring the feeling of the numinous into our worship?

As soon as we frame that last question, we realize the sheer impertinence of even asking it. The 'feeling of the numinous' is the human side of a divine revelation, and it is not for us to expect to manufacture it to order, or to manipulate it within the confines of liturgical engineering. The numinous blows where it lists, and we cannot dare to command it. The ways of its coming are manifold and unpredictable.

There are many avenues to moments of mystical insight.[1] For some people (and the classic example is Wordsworth) they are a commonplace of their childhood and only begin to become more rare as

> Shades of the prison-house begin to close
> Upon the growing Boy. . . .
> The Youth . . . is Nature's priest,
> And by the vision splendid
> Is on his way attended;
> At length the Man perceives it die away,
> And fade into the light of common day.[2]

Thomas Traherne was like this. We recollect that marvellous passage near the beginning of the third of his *Centuries* where he speaks of his childhood experience of 'fields of orient and immortal wheat, that never had been sown, nor ever would be reaped', and tells us how rarely he was able as an adult to recapture that childhood ecstasy.

Others are different. They are surprised in adult life by an experience they never knew as children, an experience which comes to them in 'the unattended moment' during nothing more significant than a fit of distraction. They may be swept up into ecstasy in the middle of a church service or act of formal worship, or they may discover their numinous moment within the apparently secular setting of natural or man-made beauty. Loveliness of form or sound—flowers or trees, a windswept crag, sunset and seaside, a haunting melody—can take a man outside himself and flood his soul with the realization that there are things beyond his seeing or touching or handling; can give him what T. S. Eliot described as 'a tremour of bliss, a wink of heaven, a whisper'.[3]

Those are not the only avenues. Sometimes, this numinous awareness comes to a man at a time of failure or despair, when he is at the end of his human tether. A man may be in a situation of basic need—it may be bankruptcy, or divorce, or bereavement, or when he comes to the rock-bottom acknowledgement that he is helpless in the grip of alcoholism, or at the moment when he realizes that he has some incurable illness and his own life has not got much further left to run. He comes up against the harsh facts about the ephemera of human esteem or the unreliability of human nature or the transitoriness of human life. Then, *de profundis*, there wells up within him the feeling that if there is the impermanent, the imperfect, the transitory, then somehow, somewhere, there must be the permanent, the perfect, the eternal. There comes to him what Bishop Ian Ramsey was wont to speak of as a 'disclosure'; an apprehension of the transcendent which hides behind the visible face of sensory awareness.

The variety of avenues towards numinous awareness and the unpredictability of its coming do not stop people from going in search of it. Some people are not content that the transcendent should steal upon them unawares. They go to meet it—through prayer, through the techniques of transcendental meditation, through the dangerous avenue of a drug-induced psychedelic state. Sometimes they are successful. Often they are not. When they are not, they are tempted to despair, supposing that they are missing out on something they ought to try a little harder to cultivate, or imagining that because they cannot come by a numinous experience, their apprehension of the world is that much more superficial than that of the mystics.

They should not be dismayed. Some people live in an almost constant state of numinous awareness. Others go a whole lifetime and know it, if at all, only at second-hand through the writings of people who have left accounts of it. God has made us all different, and deals with us in different ways. On the night of his 'spiritual awakening', John Wesley was tempted to believe that there was a standard set of experiences which were the common lot of everybody whose faith had newly come alive. Because in his case there were none of the transports of joy which he had expected, he began to doubt the reality of his experience. Fortunately, he was soon taught that

> as to the transports of joy that usually attend the beginning of [faith], especially in those who have mourned deeply, God sometimes giveth, sometimes withholdeth them, according to the counsels of His own will.[4]

A man is surprised by joy. The thing about religious experience is that whatever apprehension comes to people, and by whatever avenue it is reached, it has its own sovereign freedom. It cannot be commanded or manipulated. It comes unbidden and cannot be forced. That is part of the mystery of mystery.

Above all, we must insist that numinous feeling is not an *essential* of the life of religion. It is not an end of worship, but a bonus which God sometimes gives and sometimes withholds, according to his own counsels. We cannot insist on it as a precondition of worship, nor can we hope that our worship will deliver it to order like the goods out of a slot-machine. We seek, not religious experience, but God. Because of the paradox of worship, we should not speak so much of man's quest for the transcendent as of the transcendent's search for man, man who flees him down the nights and down the days but yet, some time, some mysterious 'how', finds himself grasped by a seeking power that will brook a human denial no longer. Religious experience comes when it is least expected, often when it seems least prepared-for. I remember it flooding upon me as I stood at the back of a bare and undistinguished church one Sunday evening towards the end of the hymn after the sermon, and saw the back of an old lame sidesman as he hobbled towards the sanctuary with the collection plate, and I thought of what Christ our Lord had meant to him throughout a long life of manual toil.

> To those who know a little of christian history [once wrote Dom Gregory Dix] probably the most moving of all the reflections it brings is not the thought of the great events and the well-remembered saints, but of those innumerable millions of entirely obscure faithful men and women . . . [who] have left no slightest trace in this world, not even a name, but have passed to God utterly forgotten by men. . . . There is a little ill-spelled ill-carved rustic epitaph of the fourth century from Asia Minor:—'Here sleeps the blessed Chione, who has found Jerusalem for she prayed much'. Not another word is known of Chione, some peasant woman who lived in that vanished world of christian Anatolia. But how lovely if all that should survive after sixteen centuries were that one had prayed much, so that the neighbours who saw all one's life were sure one must have found Jerusalem![5]

That old lame sidesman is now no longer with us. From what I knew of his life, I am sure that he too has found Jerusalem. But why was it that the sight of his retreating back as he took the plate up to the Vicar, triggered off in one of the congregation that overwhelming sense of the reality of God? Truly, the numinous cannot be commanded. It came to Charles Raven (as Ian Ramsey once memorably reminded us)[6] as he passed a back-street fish-and-chip shop in Liverpool. How can our worship ever hope to compete with *that*?

It cannot; but that does not absolve us from the duty of trying so to order our worship that the numinous has the best chance of finding us in a receptive mood. That is part of the paradox of the 'I, yet not I, but God', which characterizes the care and prayer we put into the planning of our worship. For every Charles Raven who has said, 'All of a sudden, the glory . . .' outside a Liverpool fish-and-chip shop, how many dozens of people have said it during Choral Evensong at Durham Cathedral, how many hundreds at the family Eucharist at their parish church? As Otto said, 'though God indeed comes where and when He chooses, yet He will choose to come when we sincerely call upon Him and prepare ourselves truly for His visitation'.[7] How can we be sensitive to the possibility of the numinous moment? How may the careful preparation and planning of our worship facilitate God's coming to the human heart, and speak to the worshippers of the mystery of the Almighty?

Before we can answer those questions, we need to try and describe this apprehension of the numinous, and the stages through which it passes. As an experience, it is the raw material of religious awareness. It is not specifically Christian so much as basically and elementally human. For most of the time, we are unaware that we live in a world of mystery, and there does not seem to be anything hidden behind the surface of things seen. Then the moment comes in which the breeze stirs and the veils shift and something happens to our consciousness so that the world we see appears to have what Teilhard de Chardin called a 'within' as well as an exterior. These moments are almost impossible to describe, for our normal language does not seem designed for them. Wordsworth did his best, in those lines of his which he wrote as he sat on a grassy bank of the River Wye a few miles above Tintern Abbey. 'I have felt', he confessed,

> A presence that disturbs me with the joy
> Of elevated thoughts; a sense sublime
> Of something far more deeply interfused,
> Whose dwelling is the light of setting suns,
> And the round ocean, and the living air,
> And the blue sky, and in the mind of man.[8]

Often, all we can do is to use analogy or metaphor in the hopes that what we are talking about can be recognized by those who have had similar experiences. The numinous cannot be described; it can only be evoked.

As an experience, the numinous is theologically neutral. If it comes to religiously-minded man, or in a religious setting, then it may be overlaid with symbols from religious ideology, as it was for Isaiah when he described what he felt in terms of the LORD high and lifted up, surrounded by living creatures and a ceaseless sound of 'Holy, Holy, Holy'; or as it was for an exile in a strange land on the Lord's day, who wrote down what he saw as the Book of the Revelation to John. If it comes to secularized man, or in a secular setting, it can just as easily be brushed off as emotion, or a quirk of physiochemistry, and laughed away into the harsh lethal light of common day.[9]

Those who do not wish to laugh it away, however, believe that although moments like this do not come often, nor do they last long, yet their significance does not depend on their duration or their frequency. They are seconds of truth, moments of significance, crowded hours of glorious life which can tell us more about the mystery of the world than all the rest of our ages without name. Some people use moments like this to say (as Jacob said when he had his moment of numinous awareness in the dream of the ladder full of the angels of God ascending and descending upon it), 'Truly the LORD is in this place, and I did not know it' (Gen. 28.16). They can use the experience as a starting-point for a pilgrimage towards the God whom they have thus mystically and half-consciously apprehended.

There are two moments to (or aspects of) the numinous experience which are of particular importance in relation to our worship. In that seminal book of his, *The Idea of the Holy*, Rudolf Otto characterized the numinous as *mysterium tremendum*, but then went on to describe the way in which this *tremendum* was accompanied by a complementary feeling, one of being drawn towards or fascinated by the *mysterium*. We will do well to keep the phrase *mysterium tremendum et fascinans* in mind as we explore the relation of our worship to the mystery of numinous awareness.

The first movement is the realization of the *overwhelming* nature of the mystery of which we have become aware. It is so great, so tremendous, that our instinct is to cringe before it in self-abasement, realizing our sinful incongruity in the face of the otherworldly holiness of which we have caught so terrifying a glimpse. So Isaiah cried out, 'Woe is me! I am lost, for I am a man of unclean lips and I dwell among a people of unclean lips; yet with these eyes I have seen the King, the LORD of Hosts' (Isa. 6.5). Peter, after the miraculous draught of fishes, when he had realized that in Jesus of Nazareth there was something more than the merely human, exclaimed, 'Go, Lord, leave me, sinner that I am!' (Luke 5.8). We hasten to put a safe distance between ourselves and the *mysterium tremendum*, for has not God said, 'No mortal man may see me and live' (Exod. 33.20)?

Yet things cannot stop there. If *mysterium tremendum* is at one pole of the numinous awareness, here is yet another place where we come across paradox, for at the other pole there is *mysterium fascinans*. Try as we may to distance ourselves from the terror of the numinous moment, its fascination, its drawing-power, will inexorably pull us back towards the Divinity whom we find we cannot live without. There is a lovely example of this in C. S. Lewis' children's book *The Lion, The Witch and the Wardrobe*. In the allegory, Aslan is the type of Christ, and Susan asks, 'Is he—quite safe?' Mrs Beaver replies

'If there's anyone who can appear before Aslan without their knees knocking, they're either braver than most or else just silly.'

'Then he isn't safe?' said Lucy.

'Safe?' said Mr Beaver; 'don't you hear what Mrs Beaver tells you? Who said anything about safe? 'Course he isn't safe. But he's good. He's the King, I tell you.'

'I'm longing to see him,' said Peter, 'even if I do feel frightened when it comes to the point.'[10]

'It is a terrible thing to fall into the hands of the living God' (Heb. 10.31), but it is more terrible still to fall *out* of those hands, for his majesty is equalled by his mercy (Ecclus. 2.18).

We find, then, that this God who terrifies us, will not let us go. Jeremiah who determined not to speak any more in God's name found it in his heart as it were a burning fire shut up in his bones so that he could not contain himself (Jer. 20.9). Isaiah found an angel with a burning coal cauterizing his sinful lips, and heard a cry in response to which he could not prevent himself from becoming a volunteer (Isa. 6.6–8). Peter who had tried to distance himself from the holiness of Jesus, grasped the helping hand and was called to become a fisher of men (Luke 5.10). When Elijah on Horeb heard that low numinous sound, as of a gentle murmuring, and hid his face in his cloak because he knew it was his LORD and his God speaking to him, the call was to continue to work for God and to co-operate with him in the political structures of the world, however bloody the outcome:

> Go back by way of the wilderness of Damascus, enter the city and anoint Hazael to be king of Aram; anoint Jehu son of Nimshi to be king of Israel, and Elisha son of Shaphat of Abel-Meholah to be prophet in your place. Anyone who escapes the sword of Hazael Jehu will slay, and anyone who escapes the sword of Jehu Elisha will slay. (1 Kings 19.15–17)

The numinous is at one and the same time *mysterium tremendum* and *mysterium fascinans*. If our worship is to partake of the dimension of the numinous, both these awarenesses must be allowed for. The community of the faithful must enter into what the Prayer Book collect of the Second Sunday after Trinity describes as the 'perpetual fear [*mysterium tremendum*] and love [*mysterium fascinans*] of [God's] holy Name'. How can we help our congregations enter into the mystery of worship?

We do it by making sure that our rite expresses the truth we have apprehended with the maximum of clarity and precision. That may be a surprising thing to say, but the paradox of the Christian mystery is that it is an open mystery, not a concealed one. God is a *revealing* God; and 'he has made known to us in all wisdom and insight the mystery of his will' (Eph. 1.9 R.S.V.), so that Paul can pray 'that utterance may be given me in opening my mouth boldly to proclaim the mystery of the gospel' (Eph. 6.19 R.S.V.). We are those to whom it has been given to know the mysteries of the kingdom of heaven (Matt. 13.11, Luke 8.10).

> There are mysteries which darken and conceal [wrote Michael Richards]; and there are mystics whose search for a refuge from

the world and from themselves requires the hatred of both [the world and themselves]; the perennial gnostic and the everlasting manichee. There are liturgies that we have made mysterious by turning them protectively into linguistic monuments. Before we put our worship into words and music, ritual and vestment, we must be sure that we know and begin to understand the true nature of the mystery we celebrate. . . . Christianity took the term 'mystery' and developed its meaning, making it stand now not for secrecy, obscurity or concealment, but for declaration and making plain. The plan of God for the world was at one time hidden from man and inaccessible; but now he has committed himself to a course of action within human society which he has announced and explained.[11]

In other words, 'those who have incarnation, crucifixion, and resurrection to proclaim need no humanly created veils in which to shroud their mysteries'.[12] The danger in liturgy is that we may allow a false mystification to prevent us from seeing the true mystery of the gospel. We may allow the patina of age to hide from us the burnished glow of the new-minted metal. A false reverence for ancient words or hallowed formulae may make it impossible for the true religious moment to occur. We may find ourselves in danger of worshipping a figment of our own psychology, a squirt of hormone into the bloodstream, what Michael Richards called 'the catch in the throat', when we ought to be face to face with the reality of Jesus Christ himself.

Alwyn Williams, the former Bishop of Durham who chaired the committees in charge of the New English Bible, spoke of the same thing in relation to the language of biblical translation. Let the reader go through the early chapters of Luke in the N.E.B. translation, and ask himself

whether he is still not moved by a profound sense of mystery, felt all the more sharply perhaps because it is essential mystery belonging to the story rather than the mystery of a language which we no longer use. . . . It is, after all, the translator's business to solve linguistic mysteries if he can: what I have called essential mystery lies at a deeper level.[13]

Simplicity and mystery, therefore, far from being mutually exclusive, can most profoundly coexist. There is no need to strive after effect in order to create mystery. To do so may indeed drive the divine mystery away. The human over-elaboration often needs to be stripped off before the true mystery can be apprehended. The veil of the Jerusalem Temple was a wonderful piece of human artistry. Josephus describes it as made of

> fine linen and purple, and blue, and scarlet colours; ... embroidered with all sorts of flowers which the earth produces; and there were interwoven into it all sorts of variety that might be an ornament.[14]

But it was split from end to end at the death of Christ.

> The event which instituted our great Eucharistic mystery was accompanied by artistic vandalism of the first order: God in action shattered the best that man could create to symbolize and honour God's mystery and transcendence.[15]

Through the death of Christ, the numinous place lay open to human gaze. The sacred had become profane. Now man could look: but still only God could make him see. And what he could see was not the marvel of human art and visible beauty, purple and blue and scarlet, linen and tapestry and embroidery; but the atonement between God and man at the brutal and secular point where two planks of timber made a cross.

In view of this, it would be a grievous error indeed to plan worship which consciously strives for numinous effect. We must keep ourselves open to the possibility of its occurrence, but we must realize that God can reveal himself to the heart of a worshipper at any point, whether in the ravishing music of the Elevation at the Beethoven Missa Solennis or in that procession down the aisle during Anglican Evensong in a small-town church about which we were thinking a few pages back. What is essential is that we make sure that if that numinous moment *does* happen, it happens within a rite which expresses a true theological understanding with clarity and precision.

We can make the liturgy as clear as the Holy of Holies after the splitting of the veil without emptying it of its true mystery, because its true mystery is the mystery of the confrontation of the soul with its maker, the mystery of the gospel which reveals and makes clear the hidden purpose of God, the mystery of the true stone of stumbling and rock of offence. Indeed, we owe it to the comprehensibility of the gospel to reduce mystification in order to clear the way for man to be taken hold of by the true mystery.

Let us therefore close by looking at the relation of worship to mystery under the four headings of structure, ritual, language, and familiarity.

1. *Structure*

We want the worshippers to know what they are taking part in when they join in an act of Christian worship. This is not easy to do if the worship is badly structured. When a Christian community comes together for its worship, there will be certain items on its agenda. It helps in an understanding of the rite if we can set these items out, and ensure that they are logically separated within the structure of the act of worship.

Christian worship can be thought of as having a five-fold agenda:

(*a*) to adore the majesty of God and to sing his praises;
(*b*) to listen to God's Word;
(*c*) to pray for each other and for the world;
(*d*) to cleanse the consciences of the worshippers;
(*e*) to do with the bread and wine what Jesus commanded—i.e. to take, bless, break, and share.

Not all of these items will be on the agenda for every meeting of Christians. Some of them can stand on their own, and when they do, the question of the structure of the rite or the order of events is not particularly important. Thus, sometimes Christians want to come together simply to sit under the Word of God, to read it, to tease out its message, to find its relevance to their world and situation, and to be encouraged by it in their corporate worship of the God whose Word it is. At other times, they will want to come together simply for the shared experience of prayer, praise, joy, and intercession with thanksgiving. None of these is particularly structured. It is when the fifth item is on the agenda—when Christians meet around the table with bread and wine—that all the other items need to be included as well, and the rite then becomes so complex that without a meaningful structure it can simply be confusing.

There should be no Eucharist without the Ministry of the Word and the intercessions; nor should it take place without adoration and confession. That being so, there are two things to watch. The first is that the Eucharist must have the *right* structure, so that the necessary items follow upon each other in the most worshipfully satisfactory way. The other is that it must have a *clear* structure, so that the separate items of the agenda are marked off from each other, to make it clear to the congregation where it has got to at any moment of the rite, and what precisely it is doing at any particular moment within it.

The eucharistic rite of the Book of Common Prayer is not ideal in either of these aspects. Its structure is muddled—for example, the bread and wine are put on the table as though we were about to begin the Ministry of the Sacrament, and then we promptly forget all about them as we go off into intercessions, confession, and absolution before picking up the thread again. Nor is its order of events ideal. The Prayer of Humble Access, in the opinion of many people, imparts a penitential note at too late a stage in the service, when we should be well advanced into our crescendo of praise and thanksgiving which begins with the Sursum Corda, via the Preface, to the eucharistic Prayer.

Some people would positively defend a lack of logical order within a service, claiming that a neat and rational service fails the worshippers on two counts. The first is that we are not creatures of logical progression. The average worshipper has a very short span of concentration, and his attention is not easily riveted by the kind of service which lumbers along like a logical juggernaut. Our television commentators, newscasters, and programme directors know perfectly well that an abrupt change of voice, tone, or subject-matter does not necessarily confuse. It may give the mind which is tired of a long and careful logical progression, time to relax and be refreshed. This is true, but it need not be overstressed. It does not tell us to abandon structural good sense altogether in the planning of a service. What it *does* do is to warn us against turning it into a shibboleth.

The other count on which the rationally-planned service is condemned is that it destroys any chance of the numinous moment occurring. We had better hear Otto himself on this subject, because though his words were written sixty years ago, they have a curiously modern ring, foreshadowing those people who despair of making Series 3 a vehicle of numinous mystery. Otto was writing of 'the remaining portions of the old Mass which recur[red] in the Lutheran ritual' of his day, and he went on to say about them that

> just because their design shows but little of regularity or conceptual arrangement, they preserve in themselves far more of the spirit of worship than the proposed recastings of the service put forward by the most recent practical reformers. In these we find carefully arranged schemes worked out with the balance and coherence of an essay, but nothing unaccountable, and for that very reason suggestive; nothing accidental, and for that very reason pregnant in meaning; nothing that rises from the deeps below consciousness to break the rounded unity of the wonted disposition, and thereby point to a unity of a higher order—in a word, little that is really spiritual.[16]

Powerful words; but we must not forget that Otto sub-titled his book 'An Inquiry into the non-rational factor in the idea of the divine . . .'. He was speaking of the irrational aspect of the numinous, and we have been at pains to argue that in Christian worship, the numinous must not be sought for its own sake, but as an elemental experience which needs to be set within, and purified by, a Christian *understanding* of God. The unstructured rite containing the irrational apprehension can so easily foster the kind of worship which shrinks from any attempt to wrestle with the understanding of the true Christian mystery. A modern, well-planned service can lead those who participate in it to so deep an understanding of what Christian faith and Christian worship are about, that it triggers off for them the most profound kind of numinous experience, an experience in which head as well as heart is touched, renewed, and converted.

The most satisfactory structuring of our worship is one which mirrors the pattern of the numinous moment itself. This is exactly what the revised eucharistic rites do. The shape of the eucharistic liturgy can be described in terms of *mysterium tremendum et fascinans*.

The first moment in worship should not be a reminder of our sinfulness and a call to penitence. That is the mistake of the Prayer Book offices of Mattins and Evensong.[17] The first movement should be to become aware of God; if that happens, then a sense of our own unworthiness will arise unbidden. The eucharistic rite is patterned exactly in this way. First we sing the *Gloria in Excelsis*, praising, worshipping, and glorifying God in highest heaven. Then we put ourselves under the Word of God in scripture and sermon and follow this by praying for the needs of the whole world. It is only in the light of the majesty of God's *mysterium tremendum*, of the facts of his self-revelation in holy Scripture, and in a knowledge of the needs of all creation (brought home to us by the intercessions) that our sinful inability to rise to what we have been called to be, becomes so apparent that confession can no longer be held off.[18]

When we have become aware of the overarching majesty of God and, contrasted against it, our own sinfulness and unworthiness, the numinous paradox begins to unfold. We ought to be terrified, but instead we are fascinated. This great mystery is drawing us. We cannot escape it, nor have we any desire to do so. After confession we draw close to the *mysterium fascinans*. We enter *illud tempus*, the mystical moment at the centre of the history of salvation. We go out of profane time with its errors and limitations, and into a sacred time in which time itself is transcended. We stand once more at that moment when Jesus Christ, on the night in which he was betrayed, took bread and, when he had given thanks to God, broke it and gave it to his disciples, saying, 'Take, eat'. If we find that the mystery draws us to himself, then we can never draw closer than when we take that mystery into our very bodies as bread and wine. The *mysterium fascinans* then becomes the motive power whereby we are sent out once more—like Isaiah, like Peter, like Elijah—into the secular world, the world outside the numinous mystery, the world which is to be transformed and converted by the power that we have taken into ourselves:

> Send us out
> in the power of your Spirit
> to live and work
> to your praise and glory.[19]

2. Ritual

The Protestant Englishman, with his horror of Papalistic ritualism, dies hard. Yet we cannot escape ritual, for the service must be presented in *some* outward and physical form, however unplanned the gesture and movement may be. We have already seen (pages 23–4 above) that the way in which we arrange the service and even the geography of the church interior can speak to the worshippers more loudly than the words of the service, so it is important to be aware of this, in order to ensure that the right message is spoken by this means.

Ritual is inescapable. It is also exceedingly powerful. It has the function of forming or expressing or creating community. It acts as a boundary between a community and the rest of the world. This is an aspect of ritual which bites deep into society, at all intellectual and cultural levels. Think of the ritual aspects of the last night of the Proms, or the Cup Final, or the Durham Miners' Gala with the Trades Union Miners' Lodge banners flying in the wind as the brass bands lead the colliers and their families past the Labour leaders on the balcony. These are emotive occasions: and the emotion is shared by the crowd because they realize that this is the way in which they, as Promenaders, or Cup Final spectators, or Durham mineworkers express and effect their solidarity as a distinctive group over against the amorphous mass of ordinary society. The same is true of civic pomp, Trooping the Colour, Freemasonry, or Rotary. Even the counter-cultural revolutionaries challenge convention by ritual activity. Provided at least one other person who is 'doing his own thing' is doing the same as you, or dropping out of society in an identical way, you and he have formed a group, and there is cohesion in it which will strengthen the individual and enable him to survive in a hostile environment or to retain his differentia in an apathetic one.

Once ritual has become established, it has the reassuring power of telling its users that things are being done in the 'right' way—viz.: in the usual, anticipated way. The child sleeps securely after the bed-time ritual has been completed—the bath, the story, the drink, the tucking-up, the bed-time kiss. He faces the world securely when the morning's similar rituals have been observed. In this, there is little element of rationality. Once established (for whatever reason) the ritual satisfies because it stands for that stability within a threatening and changing environment which enables the participant to maintain his equilibrium. Therein lies the danger of liturgical ritual: the danger of ossification. A particular way of doing things becomes stereotyped and is continued unchanged through changing societies until it is meaningless; but the suggestion that it should be altered or abandoned leads to the fiercest (because the most irrational) furore. The original meaning or symbolic significance of an action or a way of proceeding is forgotten, and all sorts of pseudo-meanings are invented in order to explain why things are done in a particular way, and why it is unthinkable that they should be done otherwise. So the devotees get incredibly upset if the acolyte snuffs the altar candles in the wrong order, or if the thurifer censes the people before he has censed the choir. That kind of ritual is external, and humanly created, and it is as fertile as a bed of weeds. It can grow ever more and more complicated and require ever more and more sophistication of its Master of Ceremonies; but it has the desired effect of separating off the 'true' Catholic from the person who does not share in the exact ritual of his less enlightened brother. We need to beware of ritual which separates more effectively than it unites.

Ritual, of course, can have its neurotic aspect. It can become obsessional, and degenerate into a pose as rational as touching every railing on the walk to work, or not walking on the cracks between the paving-stones. Then, ritual becomes a shell to hide behind, a retreat from society, an irrational funk-hole.[20] We should not be surprised that this can happen. It only proves that ritual is an integral part of everyday living, and is just as subject to the dangers of perversion as any other normal activity. It is an essential human proclivity of great power. If that power goes awry, the danger is all the greater. If it is harnessed properly, it can be an enriching thing. Ritual lies close to 'the roots of identity, meaning, belonging and communication in human life'.[21] 'The celebration of ritual expresses unconscious desires and attitudes of the participants, and helps to make them conscious'.[22] We must never suppose we can eliminate ritual or symbolism from our worship. What is essential is that we should be aware of our rituals and what they symbolize in order that they may remain healthy and theologically reputable.

That gives us the clue as to what kind of ritual renewal we should be aiming for. It should be a ritual linked with the way in which the structure of the service has been newly clarified, one where the structure is pointed up by meaningful stage-management, and where the eucharistic agenda has become the eucharistic drama.

The service to which most of us were accustomed in our younger days was a static one. If it was Mattins, it was conducted from the prayer-desk, with brief forays to the lectern and a more extended one to the pulpit at the appropriate time. If it was the Communion, it was all done from the Table. Nowadays we are used to having the Word read and expounded at the Eucharist from the desk, lectern, and pulpit, the intercessions conducted from the 'body of the kirk', and the Table left severely alone until we are ready to begin the explicitly eucharistic part of the service. This is common sense, and uses church furnishings for their intended purpose, but it has involved a real revolution in our worship. C. B. Naylor supposes a visitor from about the turn of the century arriving (by some kind of time-machine) at a present-day Eucharist. He discovers, in the considerable use now made of movement and position,

> a sense of drama which is something of a novelty to him. Before this, worship had seemed to him largely a matter of words—speaking and listening, with a minimum of movement. But this is a mixture of words and actions on equal terms. The actions moreover do not remind him at all of the kind of ceremonial he used to hear condemned as ritualism. Here the movements and changes of position seem naturally to mark the various stages of the drama, and to outline the shape of the service.[23]

This kind of ritual has not destroyed mystery, but exposed it. Inessential mystification has been stripped away from the service, so that its true mystery can be laid bare. The function of ritual is to make the meaning of the service as a whole more transparent to the worshippers, so that they can the more readily realize with its help what it is they are doing as they make Eucharist. Mystery and ritual go together: but we must not mistake what we mean when we use either term.

3. *Language*

We have often heard it said that our modern-language liturgies have destroyed the numinous quality of worship. On the appearance of Series 3 Morning and Evening Prayer, an article by Ronald Payne in the *Daily Telegraph* (25 October 1975) complained that 'committees of churchmen are busily at work dousing the literary fire in the belly of the Christian religion by re-writing and watering down the rich old prose so closely associated with godliness'. The charge reminds me of Keats' lament over the way in which the discovery of the principle of the splitting of white light by a prism destroyed for him the splendour of the rainbow as a sign of God's graciousness after the storm:

> There was an awful rainbow once in heaven:
> Wĕ know her woof, her texture; she is given
> In the dull catalogue of common things.
> Philosophy will clip an Angel's wings.[24]

Have modern services taken liturgy into the dull catalogue of common things? Have they silenced for us the beat of the wings of the angels? Has the loss of majesty, weight, and rhythm meant a loss of contact with the living springs of devotion?

We must be careful lest we limit the numinous power of language to the formula, the sentence, or even to the phrase. The numinous can be evoked in a profounder way through a single word or even a single syllable than it often can through a whole incantation. Certain words and sounds have in themselves the seeds of holy mystery. Otto himself drew attention to some of them:

As is a primitive sound to express the '*stupendum*', the long-protracted open vowel of wonder (ā, oh, hā), combining with the sibilant, which in all languages is used to express or produce a terrified silence (cf. Hist! Sh! Sst!). . . . We can detect in this word just the original 'shudder' of numinous awe in the first and earliest form in which it expressed itself, before any figure of speech, objective representation, or concept had been devised to explicate it. . . . Another original sound in which the numinous feeling is articulated is certainly the holy syllable '*om*'.[25]

That holy syllable *ōm* is of particular significance in Eastern devotion, and Tony Duncan explains why.

In Tantric Yoga there are a great many Sanscrit words, ending with the letter 'm' which are known as *Bijas*. . . . In the chanting of Bijas, the terminal 'm' is, as it were, held back (rather in the manner of an English 'ng' ending) and made to resonate *within*. . . . The nervous system, once trained to respond to the resonance of a Bija, brings the body into deep silence almost as soon as the adept begins to chant. The schools of Transcendental Meditation . . . use this kind of technique. . . . In Sufi meditation the Arabic 'll'—as in Allah—is found to have a similar psycho-physical effect to the Sanscrit 'm'—as in ōm. Early Jewish mysticism knew a similar technique in the devotional repetition of the letters of the Hebrew alphabet—adding up to the Name of God—and it is more than likely that the familiar 'Amen' had, originally, a Tantric Yoga significance![26]

The fourteenth-century English mystic who wrote the *Cloud of Unknowing* was certainly aware of the numinous value of certain words. In Chapters 7 and 39 of his work, he suggests that we should meditate on the word 'God' or the word 'love'—a syllable only; 'if I could find any shorter words . . . then I would have used those and left these'.[27]

To speak personally, I find the '*ō*' range of syllables to have a peculiar numinous power, particularly if prefixed by the aspirate, the catch in the breath whereby the numinous is characterized—'I opened my mouth, and drew in my breath: for my delight was in thy commandments' (Ps. 119.131, P.B.V.). So we get the numinous words 'Lord' or 'glory' or—supremely—'holy'. And these are the words with which worship dare not dispense, however the language is modernized.

With this as background, we can now move on to ask what is required of a service in modern language. The purpose of using contemporary speech is the same as that of using a clearly-structured rite. It is that of spelling out more perspicuously our understanding of what is happening in our worship. The questions to ask of new rites are such questions as

Are the present alterations a better expression of the reality in which worshippers are to be involved? Do they get rid of false mystification so as to confront people with the real mystery? Have they succeeded in straining off any comforting but obscure phrases which may act as sedatives or shields from the true power and glory of God?[28]

If the old rite is purchasing worship at the cost of intelligibility, it needs to be changed.

Not, however, into flat, unevocative language. We have spoken of the danger of erecting a linguistic monument, of mistaking the glow of feeling at fine Elizabethan cadences for the numinous awareness of God. Yet beauty *is* an avenue for worship, and we cannot simply produce a tawdry or a banal substitute and expect it to be as effective in creating an atmosphere of worship as is the hallowed formula which has come down to us through the centuries and speaks to us of that which transcends time. The language of worship needs to be somewhat heightened from that of common speech. It is a specialist use of language and it is not possible simply to take breakfast-table or bar-parlour conversation as a linguistic criterion of 'modern speech' for liturgical use. Far better take modern poetry. Liturgical language must have rhythm, dignity, assonance. It must be proper to its subject-matter. A good test will be whether it tempts composers to put it to music. Some geniuses can turn the most incompetent librettist into an excuse to open heaven for us, but on the whole, liturgical language is no better than the music it inspires.

The language of our liturgy must be such as to express the mystery of our religion. That requires, not only clarity, but richness; and that poses us with a problem. It was von Hügel[29] who drew the distinction between richness of thought and language—that which might appear obscure through the excess of its subject-matter over the intellectual constructions which attempt to explore it—and clarity, in which the tools of thought are entirely adequate for their purpose. We must strive for clarity in our expression if we are not to substitute 'mere puzzles which tease and hurt the mind' for 'genuine mysteries which liberate the spirit';[30] but we shall inevitably find that the richness of our subject-matter is such that the only adequate language is that which can be applied to more than one level at a time.

We are not here referring to that synodical kind of liturgical ambiguity which attempts to find a formula which will paper over the cracks of theological controversy by being read in different ways by different schools of churchmanship. We have had enough of that in recent years in relation (for instance) to the eucharistic offering, the eucharistic sacrifice, and prayers for the departed. No. What is wanted is that the language of the rite should be 'clear and many-layered, so that priest and congregation may return to it and find further meaning after many repetitions'.[31] That involves a richness of allusion which is rarely able to be achieved at the same time as simplicity of language. One example where this seems to have been successfully accomplished is the revision of the post-communion prayer of 1662 in Series 2. The Prayer Book version is:

> for that thou dost vouchsafe to feed us, who have duly received these holy mysteries, with the spiritual food of the most precious Body and Blood of thy Son our Saviour Jesus Christ; and dost assure us thereby of thy favour and goodness towards us; and that we are very members incorporate in the mystical body of thy Son, which is the blessed company of all faithful people.

In Series 2 this has become

> We thank thee that thou dost feed us in these holy mysteries with the Body and Blood of thy Son our Saviour Jesus Christ, and that thou dost keep us thereby in the Body of thy Son, which is the blessed company of all faithful people.

The new form has halved the number of words between the mention of Christ's eucharistic Body and his Body the Church. The conciseness has helped point up the double reference and make it more obvious. The mystery of the relation between Christ's body the Church and his body in the Eucharist is no less profound; but it has been made more manifest by the simplification and clarification of the language. It is in this kind of way that the use of contemporary language can deepen, rather than destroy, the mystery of worship.

4. *Familiarity*

Over the last decade or so there has been an almost constant process of liturgical revision in the Church of England. Its aim has been to provide today's congregations with worship whose structure, ritual, and words can provide a vehicle for the communication to us of the divine mystery which lies beyond human apprehensions. The tragedy of man today is that he has so few opportunities of adoration. Mystery lies all around him, but it is largely unperceived. The ancient liturgies still have their numinous power, but the danger is that they may bring the worshipper only as far as the moment of emotive realization and that he will be satisfied with that. He may stick there, and not move on to the exploration of the nature, works, and purpose of the unknown God who speaks to him in the numinous moment. If they are doing their job properly, the new rites can—by their very novelty—give the worshippers the chance of going beyond the numinous moment to a true confrontation with God as Christians have come to understand him.

There is value, therefore, in a fresh-minted liturgy. Our final question must be, How often can we renew our worship by revising our services? How much liturgical change can a man take?

We have argued (see pages 49–52) for the set rather than the extempore liturgy. It is part of the paradox which we have been discovering all through our exploration into worship that true freedom can only be found within the constraints of structure. 'Freedom and spontaneity *emerge from* structure. Structure inhibits relationships, or intrudes between persons, only when it is not understood and acknowledged'.[32] This freedom is not immediately apparent. If we are to discover the value of structured worship and a set liturgy, we must allow time for the liturgy to do its work upon us. The first time it is heard, a new liturgy is less effective than a time of extempore prayer, because a liturgy is more contrived, more formal, more literary, less spontaneously the free product of the present moment and the present congregation. It needs to be lived into. A Christian worshipper from one of the liturgical traditions of Christendom has (in part at any rate) been made into the kind of Christian he is by the liturgy in which he has participated over the years. The liturgy needs to become so familiar to the worshipper that its cadences are as natural as breathing and its words a part of a man's own self. His relation to the liturgy needs to become like the choir's relation to the music; no longer an external relation, but a co-participation so that it can be said that the music

> is not heard at all, but you are the music
> While the music lasts.[33]

When the words of the liturgy have eaten into the soul of the worshipper, the rite itself can be the ground-bass on which the multitudinous harmonies of Christian worship and devotion can be built.

That takes time. We have gone through a decade of liturgical ferment such as the Anglican church has not known since the 1540s and 1550s. Now, as after the former period of liturgical reformation, it is time to call a halt, so that we can gather our thoughts together, and pray our hearts into a liturgy which will last us a generation.

We have worked hard for the last few years on the human side of the paradox of worship. We have done our best to build up rites which can adequately express our theology, our community, and our mission, and which can point us towards the mystery of the God to whom we want to ascribe the due worth. The results are imperfect. Any human vehicle for the worship of God will be imperfect. We could continue improving our new liturgies almost without cease. I believe we have now reached a stage at which we ought not to try any longer. It is now time for the other side of the paradox of worship to take over, and for us to allow God to work through the vehicle we have fashioned. We have worked out our own worship with fear and trembling. Now let us allow God to use what we have done, and to worship within us. Let us imperfect human beings now enter into our imperfect liturgies in such a way that they help our souls prepare for that perfect worship of heaven, where angels and archangels and all the holy company ceaselessly offer prayer, praise, and joy to him who, amidst the changes and chances of his creation, ever abides unchanged. To him be praise, power, dominion, and glory, unto the ages of the ages! Amen.

NOTES

CHAPTER 1

WORSHIP AND GOD

1 Colin Dunlop, *Anglican Public Worship* (S.C.M. Press, 1953), p. 13.

2 Geddes MacGregor, *The Rhythm of God: A Philosophy of Worship* (Seabury Press, New York, 1974), p. 57.

3 Roger Grainger, *The Language of the Rite* (Darton, Longman, and Todd, 1974), pp. 33 f. The quotation from Calvin is to be found in *The Institutes of the Christian Religion*, 4.14.14.

4 Grainger, op. cit., p. 36.

5 Neville Clark in *Worship and the Child: Essays by the Joint Liturgical Group*, edited by Ronald C. D. Jasper (S.P.C.K., 1975), p. 59.

6 Clark, cap. cit., p. 67.

7 Michael Perry, 'Method and Model in the Epistle to the Hebrews', *Theology* 77 (1974), p. 68.

8 Michael Perry, *Sharing in One Bread* (S.P.C.K., 1973), pp. 58 f.

9 Dunlop, op. cit., p. 16.

10 Dunlop, op. cit., p. 26.

11 Translation by Leo Sherley-Price in his Introduction to Bede's *History of the English Church and People* (Penguin Books, rev. edn 1968), p. 16.

12 John Dalrymple, *Costing Not Less than Everything* (Darton, Longman, and Todd, 1975), p. 82.

13 MacGregor, op. cit., p. 23.

14 Grainger, op. cit., p. 29.

15 Grainger, op. cit., p. 30.

16 Grainger, op. cit., p. 30. The work of Louis Bouyer to which he refers is his *Rite and Man* (Burns, Oates, 1963).

17 D. M. Baillie, *God was in Christ* (Faber and Faber, 2nd edn 1955), p. 110.

18 Baillie, op. cit., p. 117.

19 Baillie, op. cit., p. 108.

20 Baillie, op. cit., p. 114.

CHAPTER 2

WORSHIP AND BELIEF

1 An extension of a phrase of Pascal's (1623–62). His words were 'Thou wouldst not seek Me, if thou hadst not found Me', and 'Thou wouldst not seek Me, if thou didst not possess Me'. (*Pensées* 552 (3) and 554 (5), trans. W. F. Trotter (*Everyman* edn (Dent/Dutton) 1904, pp. 149, 151).)

2 Dom Gregory Dix, *The Shape of the Liturgy* (Dacre Press, Adam and Charles Black, 1945), p. 153.

3 Mark Gibbard, *Twentieth-Century Men of Prayer* (S.C.M. Press Book Club 220, 1974), pp. 105 f.

4 J. L. Houlden in *The Eucharist Today—Studies on Series 3*, ed. R. C. D. Jasper (S.P.C.K., 1974), p. 175.

5 Houlden, cap. cit., p. 171.

6 Quoted by Eric James, *The Roots of the Liturgy* (Prism Pamphlet No. 1, 1962), pp 7 f; italics original.

7 James, loc. cit., p. 7; italics original.

8 David Head, *He Sent Leanness: A Book of Prayers for the Natural Man* (Epworth Press, 1959), pp. 34, 43.

9 Quoted in Peter J. Jagger, *Bishop Henry de Candole, His Life and Times* (Faith Press, 1975), p. 121.

10 Michael Ramsey, *Durham Essays and Addresses* (S.P.C.K., 1956), pp. 19 f.

11 John Riches, 'Present-day Eucharistic Spirituality', *Theology* 77 (1974), p. 175.

12 For the illustration, see Michael Perry, 'Method and Model in the Epistle to the Hebrews', *Theology* 77 (1974), p. 67.

13 R. Williamson, 'The Eucharist and the Epistle to the Hebrews', *New Testament Studies* 21 (1975), p. 310.

14 J. H. S. Kent, 'The Socinian Tradition', *Theology* 78 (1975), p. 134.

15 Geddes MacGregor, *The Rhythm of God: A Philosophy of Worship* (Seabury Press, New York, 1974), p. 85.

16 Houlden, cap. cit., p. 174.

17 Houlden, ibid., pp. 173 f.

18 Riches, art. cit., p. 180.

19 Riches, ibid.

20 John Newton (1725–1807), *Hymns Ancient and Modern Revised* No. 192, verse 4 (where Newton's 'Husband' becomes 'Brother'—itself a significant change in imagery and symbolism).

21 See in particular, 'Talking about God: Models, Ancient and Modern' by Ian T. Ramsey in S.P.C.K. *Theological Collections* 7 (1966), *Myth and Symbol*, pp. 76–97.

22 G. M. Hopkins, *God's Grandeur*.

23 J. V. Taylor, *The Go-Between God* (S.C.M. Press, 1972), p. 92.

CHAPTER 3
WORSHIP AND COMMUNITY

1 See, on this whole subject, 'New Wine in Old Wineskins: XII. Firstfruits' by Robert Murray, S.J., in *Expository Times* 86 (1975), pp. 164–8. The historicization of Passover from a nomadic ritual into a memorial of the deliverance from Egypt is also outlined by Robert Crotty in *Good News in Mark* (Collins Fontana, 1975), pp. 40–1.

2 *Pace* Murray, art. cit., p. 165, who states that 'there is no mention of the Passover sacrifice' in either of these passages.

3 Murray, ibid., p. 165.

4 Jan Milič Lochman, 'The Trinity and Human Life', *Theology* 78 (April, 1975), p. 179. His italics.

5 Thames and Hudson, 1974.

6 Geddes MacGregor, *The Rhythm of God: A Philosophy of Worship* (Seabury Press, New York, 1974), p. 40.

7 John Gunstone, *The Charismatic Prayer Group* (Hodder and Stoughton, 1975), pp. 130 f.

8 Gunstone, op. cit., p. 129.

9 Lesslie Newbigin, in 'Nairobi 1975: A Personal Report', appendix II of '*Jesus Christ Frees and Unites*' (C.I.O. 76—General Synod paper GS 285), pp. 22, 18.

10 G. R. Dunstan, *Theology* 78 (April, 1975), p. 170; his italics.

11 R. C. D. Jasper (ed.) in *The Eucharist Today—Studies on Series 3* (S.P.C.K., 1974), p. 6.

12 Jasper, ibid.

13 'Radius'—the Religious Drama Society (George Bell House, 8 Ayres Street, London SE1 1ES) is always ready to help and advise.

14 Michael Ramsey, *Durham Essays and Addresses* (S.P.C.K., 1956), p. 18.

15 Gunstone, op. cit., pp. 125, 131.

16 Trevor Lloyd, *Agapes and Informal Eucharists* (Grove Booklets on Ministry and Worship, No. 19, Grove Books 1973), pp. 16–20.

CHAPTER 4
WORSHIP AND MISSION

1 Dewi Morgan, *But God Comes First—A Meditation on the Te Deum* (Longmans, Green, 1962), p. 3.

2 Douglas Webster, *Should our Image of Mission Go?* (*Prism* pamphlet No. 15, pp. 4 f; quoted in J. G. Davies, *Worship and Mission* (S.C.M. Press, 1966), p. 31).

3 As reported by Margaret Dewey in *Thinking Mission* 5 (U.S.P.G., 1975), p. 2. See *International Review of Mission* (World Council of Churches), January 1974.

4 Dewey, ibid.

5 See Jürgen Moltmann, 'The Trinitarian History of God', *Theology* 78 (1975), pp. 632–46; especially section 2, 'The Trinity in Sending and Origin', pp. 635–8.

6 For the following paragraphs, see Michael Perry, 'Method and Model in the Epistle to the Hebrews', *Theology* 77 (1974), pp. 66–74.

7 David L. Frost in *The Eucharist Today—Studies on Series 3*, ed. R. C. D. Jasper (S.P.C.K., 1974), p. 143.

8 Eucharistic references in *Hebrews* are shrunk to vanishing-point by R. Williamson in 'The Eucharist and the Epistle to the Hebrews', *New Testament Studies* 21 (1975), pp. 300–12, but the article is a valuable conspectus of scholarly discussion on the topic.

9 P. R. Ackroyd in *Peake's Commentary on the Bible*, ed. Matthew Black and H. H. Rowley (Nelson, 1962), section 568k (p. 651)—ad loc. Zech. 8.23.

10 See C. L. Feinberg in *The New Bible Dictionary*, ed. J. D. Douglas (Inter-Varsity Fellowship, 1962), page 1228, sub voc. 'Synagogue'.

11 David L. Edwards, *Jesus for Modern Man* (Collins Fontana, 1975), p. 121.

12 Ibid. See also ibid., p. 122.

13 The terminology here is taken from Davies, op. cit., p. 25, though I have not followed Professor Davies' exact use of these terms.

14 Choan-Seng Song, 'From Israel to Asia—a Theological Leap', *Theology* 79 (1976), p. 94.

15 From the *Church Times* for 30 September 1966.

16 Trevor Beeson, *Discretion and Valour: Religious Conditions in Russia and Eastern Europe* (Collins Fontana, 1974).

17 Walter J. Hollenweger reviewing Trevor Beeson's book in the *Expository Times* 86 (1975), p. 155.

18 John D. Davies, *Good News in Galatians* (Collins Fontana, 1975), pp. 15 f.

19 J. G. Davies, op. cit., esp. pp. 70–112.

20 Gibson Winter, *The Suburban Captivity of the Churches*, p. 152 (quoted in J. G. Davies, op. cit., p. 91).

21 J. G. Davies, op. cit., p. 130.

22 John D. Davies, op. cit., p. 15

23 Max Thurian, *The Eucharistic Memorial. I. The Old Testament* (Eng. tr., 1960), p. 62; quoted in J. G. Davies, op. cit., p. 123.

24 Michael Perry, *Sharing in One Bread* (S.P.C.K., 1973), p. 38.

CHAPTER 5
WORSHIP AND MYSTERY

1 Michael Paffard's recent book *The Unattended Moment* (S.C.M. Press, 1976) contains a valuable selection of accounts of such experiences.

2 William Wordsworth (1770–1850), *Intimations of Immortality from Recollections of Early Childhood*, stanza 5.

3 T. S. Eliot, *Murder in the Cathedral* (Faber and Faber, 1935), Part II.

4 John Wesley's *Journal*, entry for 24 May 1738.

5 Dom Gregory Dix, *The Shape of the Liturgy* (Dacre Press, Adam and Charles Black, 1945), pp. 744 f.

6 I. T. Ramsey, *Our Understanding of Prayer* (Archbishops' Commission on Christian Doctrine Occasional Paper No. 1, S.P.C.K., 1971), p. 10.

7 Rudolf Otto, *The Idea of the Holy*, translated by J. W. Harvey (O.U.P., second edn 1950), p. 214.

8 William Wordsworth, *Lines Composed a few miles above Tintern Abbey* (13 July 1798), lines 93–9.

9 Much of the preceding pages is an expansion and reconsideration of p. 70 of 'The Quest for the Transcendent through the Paranormal', Michael Perry, *Modern Churchman* 16 (n.s.) 1972.

10 C. S. Lewis, *The Lion, the Witch and the Wardrobe* (1950), Penguin edn, p. 75.

11 Michael Richards, 'Understanding the mystery of the Christian Church', *The Times* for 28 December 1974.

12 David L. Frost, 'Liturgical Language from Cranmer to Series 3' in *The Eucharist Today*, ed. R. C. D. Jasper (S.P.C.K., 1974), p. 145.

13 A. T. P. Williams, 'Some Thoughts on Biblical Translation', a lecture delivered on the Claude Montefiore foundation in February 1962, as reprinted in C. H. G. Hopkins, *Bishop A. T. P. Williams* (Mayhew-McCrimmon, 1975), pp. 151 f.

14 Josephus, *Antiquities* 3.6.4., trans. William Whiston (1737); this refers to Moses' wilderness tabernacle, but the veil of the Herodian Temple was similar —see Josephus, *Wars of the Jews*, 5.5.4.

15 Frost, cap. cit., p. 144.

16 Otto, op. cit., p. 65.

17 Despite what I said in my earlier book, *The Pattern of Matins and Evensong* (Hodder and Stoughton, 1961), pp. 16–18.

18 That is a *rationale* of our present arrangement. The historical (and largely fortuitous) way in which it came about is retold by J. Gunstone on pp. 75 f of *The Eucharist Today*, ed. R. C. D. Jasper (S.P.C.K., 1974).

19 Holy Communion Series 3, prayer 40.

20 The psychopathological critique of ritual is dealt with at length by Roger Grainger in *The Language of the Rite* (Darton, Longman and Todd, 1974), pp. 47–77.

21 Bernice Martin, reviewing two books on ritual in *Theology* 78 (1975), p. 213.

22 Monica Wilson, *Religion and the Transformation of Society* (1971), p. 124, quoted by John Riches in 'Present-day Eucharistic Spirituality', *Theology* 77 (1974), p. 176.

23 C. B. Naylor, *Why Prayer Book Revision at All?* (C.I.O., 1964), p. 12.

24 John Keats (1795–1821), Lamia, part 2, lines 231–4.

25 Otto, op. cit., pp. 191–3.

26 A. D. Duncan, *The Fourth Dimension* (Mowbray, 1975), pp. 109–10.

27 *The Cloud of Unknowing*, ed. and trans. by Clifton Wolters (Penguin, 1961), chap. 39, p. 99.

28 Richards, art. cit.

29 Quoted in H. E. W. Turner, *Jesus the Christ* (Mowbray, 1976), pp. 130 f.

30 Gabriel Marcel, quoted in Turner, ibid.

31 Frost, cap. cit., p. 162.

32 Grainger, op. cit., p. xi; his italics.

33 T. S. Eliot, *Four Quartets: The Dry Salvages* (Faber & Faber, 1944).

INDEX OF AUTHORS CITED

115

INDEX OF SUBJECTS

INDEX OF BIBLICAL REFERENCES